TEACHING INTEGRATED STEM IN MIDDLE SCHOOL

TEACHING INTEGRATED STEM IN MIDDLE SCHOOL

S. SELCEN GUZEY

PURDUE UNIVERSITY PRESS
WEST LAFAYETTE, INDIANA

Copyright © 2025 by Siddika Selcen Guzey. All rights reserved.

Cataloging-in-Publication Data on file at the Library Congress.

978-1-62671-307-9 (paperback)

978-1-62671-308-6 (epdf)

Cover images: Science icons set—thin line, editable stroke vectors for physics, chemistry, biology research, sciences and laboratory education: PeterSnow/iStock via Getty Images Plus. STEM vector horizontal blue thin line banner or illustration: lexashka/iStock via Getty Images Plus.

To Ediz, my inspiration

CONTENTS

Preface   ix

Introduction: An Overview of the Purpose, Scope, and Significance of Integrated STEM Education   1

1. Understanding Integrated STEM Education: A Synthesis of the Literature   2

2. A Framework for Integrated STEM Education   5

3. An Instructional Guide for Developing Integrated STEM Curriculum Units   7

4. Sample Curriculum Units   15

   Designing a Two-Stage Water Filter Unit   16

      by Valarie Bogan, Shelbi Smeathers, and S. Selcen Guzey

   Designing Sunscreen Unit   44

      by Valarie Bogan, Shelbi Smeathers, and S. Selcen Guzey

5. Advancing Integrated STEM Education: Future Directions and Research Opportunities   74

Conclusion: Reflections and Implications for Practice and Policy   76

References   77

About the Author   83

PREFACE

Integrated STEM (science, technology, engineering, and mathematics) education has become a central focus of educational reforms in many countries around the world. Educators and researchers have increasingly recognized its benefits for student learning and engagement. However, many challenges have remained in achieving broad and successful implementation. Ten years ago, the main challenge was the lack of a clear and commonly accepted definition of integrated STEM education. Today, the major challenge is the limited number of high-quality, well-developed instructional resources that support effective integrated STEM instruction.

Over the years, research has shown the importance of grounding the conceptualizations and the design of integrated STEM curriculum units in well-established theories of teaching and learning. This has significantly informed the quality and coherence of STEM programs. The body of literature on integrated STEM education has grown rapidly, and numerous meta-analyses have documented various impacts of these programs on both teachers and students.

This book defines integrated STEM education from a science educator's perspective and presents a framework and instructional guide for curriculum development, along with two curriculum units. This work is rooted in research and years of experience. Over the past two decades, I have had the privilege of working and collaborating with many wonderful researchers and educators on multiple projects. Together, we have learned many things and developed a great number of curriculum units and professional development programs. We are so proud to be able to reach thousands of teachers and K–12 students through our projects.

The curriculum units shared in this book were developed as part of a project funded by the National Science Foundation (grant no. 1721141). The units could not be developed without significant classroom experiences, knowledge, and the contributions of Valarie Bogan and Shelbi Smeathers. I am deeply grateful to them both for their work in developing, field-testing, and refining the units.

It is my sincere hope that the framework, instructional guide, and curriculum units included in this book will serve as meaningful and practical resources for educators who are seeking such resources to integrate science and engineering in middle school classrooms.

INTRODUCTION: AN OVERVIEW OF THE PURPOSE, SCOPE, AND SIGNIFICANCE OF INTEGRATED STEM EDUCATION

The benefits of integrated, interdisciplinary approaches in education have been well-documented in the literature. When students engage with practices and knowledge from multiple disciplines, they learn to solve complex, real-world problems. This approach not only deepens their understanding of disciplinary content but also fosters critical thinking, problem solving, and creativity (English et al. 2017).

Integrated STEM (science, technology, engineering, and mathematics) education can take many forms (Halawa 2024; McLure et al. 2022), and various definitions of and approaches to it exist. While some researchers consider integrated STEM education to be teaching a combination of all four disciplines, others define it as teaching two or more STEM disciplines (Kelley and Knowles 2016; Moore et al. 2014; Roehrig et al. 2021). This book focuses specifically on the integration of science and engineering content and practices within middle school classrooms. By using engineering context, content, and practices, science teachers can teach science and create more meaningful and engaging learning experiences for students. In this context, integrated STEM education can be defined as the teaching of science through the lens of engineering design in culturally and socially relevant contexts.

The book is organized as follows. Chapter 1 provides a synthesis of the literature on integrated STEM education, with particular emphasis on science and engineering integration. Chapter 2 introduces a framework that was developed through both research and prior experiences in teaching integrated STEM in middle school science classrooms. This framework describes several critical elements required to design high-quality integrated STEM curricular units. Chapter 3 provides an instructional guide for curriculum development and lesson planning, building on the backward design model (Wiggins and McTighe 2005). This instructional guide supports teachers in effectively planning for lessons and curricular units, embedding content and practices from multiple disciplines.

Chapter 4 presents two sample curriculum units—one focused on designing a two-stage water filter and another on developing effective sunscreen. These units were developed as part of a curriculum and professional development project funded by the National Science Foundation. The units have been field-tested and are ready for classroom use. Chapter 5 explores future research directions and offers suggestions to further advance integrated STEM education. The conclusion reflects on key insights and discusses implications for practice and policy.

1

UNDERSTANDING INTEGRATED STEM EDUCATION: A SYNTHESIS OF THE LITERATURE

Education studies demonstrate that meaningful learning occurs when students actively engage in their learning (Halawa et al. 2020; Minner et al. 2010; NASEM, 2019). Prior research supports the use of scientific inquiry and engineering design for involving and engaging students in meaningful learning experiences (e.g., Cunningham and Kelly 2017; Pleasant and Olson 2019). Specifically, in the context of K–12 science teaching and learning, the recent education reforms in the United States and internationally (Government of Canada 2014; NRC 2012; NGSS Lead States 2013; Office of the Chief Scientist 2014) identify scientific investigations and engineering design as central components. In this new vision of science education, engineering design plays a critical role. Engineering design is a process that can be defined in several ways, yet it is commonly accepted that it is complex and requires creativity, critical thinking, and knowledge across multiple disciplines (Cunningham and Kelly 2017; Dorst 2011; NASEM 2020; Pleasant and Olson 2019). When students engage in scientific investigations and engineering design, they engage in practices such as asking questions, defining problems, collecting and analyzing data, building models, designing prototypes, devising explanations or design solutions, and communicating information and reasoning to others (NRC 2012). These practices and experiences allow students to engage in integrated instruction, making them a vital curricular addition (Cunningham et al. 2020; English and King 2019; NASEM 2019; NRC 2012).

Integrated STEM curriculum units that are organized around scientific investigations and engineering design help students build various skills. With the engineering design process, students design solutions to real-world problems; they make evidence-based decisions to progress from the first step of understanding the problem to the last step of defining an effective solution. Engaging in this highly iterative process helps students understand that design problems may have many possible solutions, and successful solutions require the application of scientific knowledge (Crismond and Adams 2012). By planning and carrying out scientific investigations to support engineering design solutions when needed, students gain an understanding of the natural and design world and see the connections between science and engineering (NASEM 2019). Design challenges often allow students to engage in engineering practices, teamwork, communication, and design thinking (García-Carmona et al. 2025).

In recent years, there has been a growing emphasis on understanding how integrated STEM curricula or teacher professional development impact student outcomes (Li et al. 2020). A review of the literature shows that integrated STEM education helps students build a robust and thorough understanding of science concepts and increases engagement, motivation, and interest in science and engineering (Cunningham et al. 2020; Guzey et al. 2017; Mehalik et al. 2008; Valtorta and Berland 2015; Wendell and Rogers 2013). For instance, a study by Anwar et al. (2022) involving middle school science teachers who received professional development in integrated STEM instruction found that the students made significant gains in science understanding after engaging in science and engineering instruction. Large-scale studies have echoed these findings. Cunningham et al. (2020) conducted a randomized trial involving a large number of elementary classrooms. Students who participated in the Engineering is Elementary project, which blends science content with engineering design, outperformed their peers in both science and engineering. Similarly, research by Capobianco and Lehman (2018) and Wendell and Rogers (2013) demonstrated that integrated STEM experiences can enhance both learning and engagement among young students. Earlier work by Fortus et al. (2004, 1082) supported the use of design pedagogies in science classrooms by documenting the positive impact of the design-based science units on students' development of scientific knowledge. According to the authors, the units were designed to "help students construct scientific understanding and real-world problem-solving skills by engaging them in the design artifacts."

Zhou et al. (2024) conducted a meta-analysis in which they investigated the impact of degree of integration (i.e., context, content, and tool integration) on student achievement. Their findings show the positive effect of integrated STEM instruction on student achievement, with context integration yielding the largest effect size followed by content integration and then tool integration. In a narrower focus, Crotty et al. (2017) studied the impact of approaches to integrating engineering in STEM units and student achievement gains. The authors found that when engineering is meaningfully, explicitly integrated into lessons within STEM curricular units rather than simply treated as an add-on project to an existing unit, higher student achievement gains in engineering are achieved.

In a recent study, Hiwatig et al. (2024) explored the impact of integrated STEM approaches on student attitudes using pre- and post-attitude surveys. The findings suggest that student engagement in engineering design and STEM content that is relevant to students' personal lives positively impacts students' attitudes toward STEM. Other research has also documented key factors that support positive student attitudes. Incorporating elements such as problem-solving, creativity (Berland and Steingut 2016), hands-on learning activities (Moore et al. 2014), the interdisciplinary nature of design activities (Guzey et al. 2016), and opportunities for collaboration and teamwork (Moore et al. 2014) into STEM instruction contributes to fostering more favorable perceptions of STEM. Researchers specializing in interest development also highlight the difference between catching and holding interest. As Mitchell (1993, 426) explains, "Catching lies in finding various ways to stimulate students, whereas the essence of holding lies in finding variables that empower students." Active engagement and participation in meaningful learning activities help students to develop lasting interest and positive attitudes.

In addition to classroom activities, student demographics play a significant role in shaping attitudes and interest development. Research has demonstrated that student demographics, including gender, ethnicity, socioeconomic status, and cultural background, shape their identities and influence their career choices (Calabrese Barton et al. 2013; Desy et al. 2011; Grossman and Porche 2014). Other studies of integrated science and engineering with students of diverse ethnic, cultural, linguistic, and economic backgrounds demonstrated that it provides a powerful opportunity for students to engage in design for the development of knowledge, skills, and identities. For example, building on students' lived experiences and community-based problems, Calabrese Barton et al. (2017) designed and implemented a makerspace program for students from minoritized communities. The authors documented that the carefully and purposefully designed STEM learning opportunities supported students' engagement. Such engagements in engineering practices and critical discourse illustrated that the program provided multiple pathways for students from low-income communities to engage in maker spaces. Taken together, it is evident that research-based pedagogies and curriculum materials play a major role in effective integrated science and engineering education for *all* students (NASEM 2020).

While the literature shows the benefits of integrated STEM education on student outcomes, implementation of such instruction remains limited. Dare et al.'s (2018) study of science teachers' implementation of integrated STEM curricular units documented three degrees of integration: low, medium, and high. The authors found that the degree of integration depends on teachers' instructional decisions and practices about the nature of integration, their choice between science and engineering, and student engagement and motivation. Making explicit or implicit connections among disciplines, balancing the focus on content from multiple disciplines, and making instruction engaging for students appear to impact teachers' degree and level of integration. Such a varied level of implementation could be also related to teachers' conceptualization of integrated STEM education (Ring-Whalen et al. 2018). Additionally, teachers' instructional goals influence the degree and level of integration of content and practices from another discipline (Dare et al. 2014). In a study in the context of a professional development program, Ring-Whalen et al. (2018) documented the alignment of teachers' conceptions of STEM and characteristics of integrated STEM curricular units that they developed. In a related study, Ring-Whalen et al. (2017) documented how teachers' conceptualizations of integrated STEM can be developed through an intensive professional development program. The study shows the importance of such professional development programs for teachers for the advancement of integrated STEM education.

Teachers face a variety of challenges when implementing integrated STEM instruction. Research has shown that many teachers, particularly science teachers, feel unprepared to teach engineering due to limited background knowledge or prior experiences (Guzey et al. 2014). Time constraints, lack of support from school and district leadership, and the unavailability of quality teaching resources for integrated STEM education further limit teachers' efforts to effectively integrate science and engineering (Dare et al. 2014, 2018; Guzey et al. 2014; Riskowski et al. 2009). Professional development programs can play a key role in addressing these challenges. Through professional development programs, teachers can explore new instructional strategies, access valuable resources and materials, and build confidence in delivering integrated STEM instruction. These experiences help teachers enhance their teaching practices. Professional development programs that provide ongoing, sustained learning opportunities are especially effective in helping teachers deepen their knowledge, improve teaching practices, and better support student learning. A recent meta-analysis by Zhou et al. (2024) found that STEM-focused professional development significantly increased teachers' self-efficacy, which is also essential for successful implementation. It is well-documented that thoughtfully designed, long-term professional development is key to broadening the implementation and impact of integrated STEM education.

2

A FRAMEWORK FOR INTEGRATED STEM EDUCATION

Recent research has demonstrated effective approaches and instructional strategies for meaningful science learning through engineering design and scientific investigations (Guzey et al. 2019; Crismond and Adams, 2012; Cunningham et al. 2020; Moore et al. 2020; NASEM 2019). A synthesis of this body of literature highlights several key characteristics of integrated science and engineering instruction: (1) having students engage in the engineering design process, (2) using engaging and motivating scientific investigations and design challenges developed around culturally and socially relevant contexts, (3) applying science content and practices to design solutions, and (4) involving students in teamwork and communication (Guzey and Li 2023). As shown in figure 2.1, all four elements are interconnected and collectively support student learning.

An *engineering design process* is a key component of engineering practices and central to engineering education in K–12 science classrooms (Crismond and Adams 2012, Dym et al. 2005; Moore et al. 2014; NASEM 2020). While many different engineering design representations are in use, Moore et al. (2014) found that

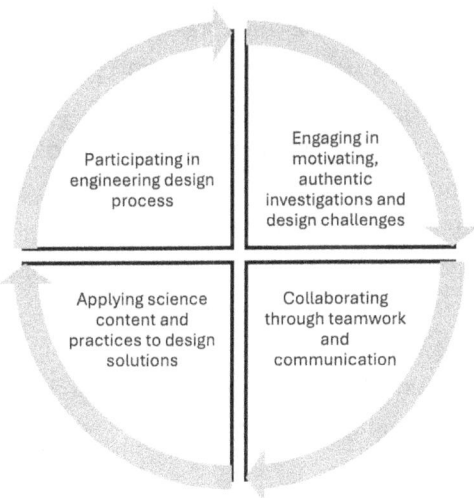

FIGURE 2.1. A framework for integrated STEM education.

engineering design processes consist of the following common indicators: understanding the problem and background, planning and implementing solutions, and testing and evaluating solutions. Although the order of these stages or activities seems sequential, the engineering design process is inherently iterative. Students often need to go back to the first phase, understanding the problem and background, as they gather information, devise solutions, and evaluate outcomes. Studies of novice versus expert designers have shown that students, as novice designers, attempt to make final design decisions too quickly and early in the design process, skip scientific investigations, spend less time on redesign, and treat design tasks as well-defined problems (Atman et al. 2007; Crismond and Adams 2012; Mentzer et al. 2015). To address these tendencies of students, Crismond and Adams (2012) suggested that teachers use strategies such as providing time for problem framing and scoping, using design briefs, enhancing students' background knowledge, and having students keep design notebooks.

Research has shown the importance of including *engaging and motivating scientific investigations and design challenges developed around culturally and socially relevant contexts* in integrated engineering and science curricular activities (Keratithamkul et al. 2020; NASEM 2019; Wilson-Lopez and Minichiello 2017). Authentic, ill-structured, contextualized, real-world design problems help students engage in issues related to their everyday lives and make science and engineering learning more meaningful (Brophy et al. 2008; Carlson and Sullivan 2004; Chin and Chia 2006; Moore et al. 2014). These engineering activities should be taught with effective pedagogies that recognize students' backgrounds, cultures, languages, and identities (Calabrese Barton et al. 2013, 2017; Cunningham and Kelly 2017; King and Pringle, 2019).

The *application of science content and practices to design solutions* is another critical element of the effective integration of science and engineering instruction (Ganesh and Schnittka 2014; Wendell et al. 2017). Students should apply science concepts relevant to the engineering design problem they are engaged in solving. When faced with an engineering problem, students often do not intentionally conduct research or scientific investigations to generate solutions. Having solid prior science content knowledge or developing a conceptual understanding of science while engaged in engineering design enables students to make evidence-based decisions and produce effective design solutions (Siverling et al. 2021; Wilson-Lopez et al. 2020). It is essential for students to understand that design involves more than aesthetic appreciation; it requires the application of scientific knowledge to design solutions. This understanding depends on teachers presenting engineering problems that are clearly connected to the science concepts being taught.

Integrated engineering design and science teaching also supports the development of twenty-first-century skills such as *teamwork* and *communication* (Crismond and Adams 2012; Cunningham and Kelly 2017; Moore et al. 2014; NRC 2010). Engaging in integrated engineering design and science investigations provides students with opportunities to collaborate and communicate effectively about their scientific data and design ideas and solutions. In engineering design teams, students work collaboratively to produce design drawings, build models, keep design portfolios, engage in reflective practices, and communicate design ideas and solutions in various formats. Engagement in science and engineering involves collaborating with peers to obtain, develop, share, and negotiate ideas, findings, and explanations. According to Cunningham and Lachapelle (2014, 126), "Collaboration and teamwork afford students rich opportunities to develop expertise and identity as valued science and engineering contributors."

3

AN INSTRUCTIONAL GUIDE FOR DEVELOPING INTEGRATED STEM CURRICULUM UNITS

Developing integrated STEM curriculum units is not an easy task. Integrating content and practices from multiple disciplines in a meaningful and engaging way for students requires detailed planning. While there are many ways to develop a quality curriculum unit, this chapter presents an instructional guide that was used to develop many integrated STEM units that were field-tested, and the impact of those on student outcomes has been well-documented.

The instructional guide involves a three-stage process based on the backward design model (Wiggins and McTighe 2005): (1) identifying desired results, (2) determining acceptable evidence, and (3) planning learning experiences and instruction. The desired results are the learning goals and objectives. Both the knowledge and the skills students should obtain at the end of the lesson or unit should be identified. These should be specific and measurable. At this stage, the state and national education standards need to be identified. An important decision for this stage is also choosing the type of approach to STEM integration. Two approaches can be used: content integration and context integration. According to Moore et al. (2014), in the content integration, multiple STEM disciplinary learning objectives are identified since the goal is teaching content and skills from different STEM areas. The context integration, on the other hand, uses context from one discipline to support the learning of the main objectives or learning goals from another discipline. The context from one discipline serves as a motivator or to make learning more realistic for students. The next step is to create assessments that can effectively measure students' learning of the intended learning outcomes. Various kinds of assessments can be used, but in the case of integrated STEM education, these assessments should closely align with learning outcomes identified for multiple disciplines. These assessments could be a combination of traditional assessments such as tests and reports as well as projects. At this stage, it is also necessary to identify an engineering challenge for the curriculum unit. This design challenge can be seen as a project that students are introduced to early in the unit that requires them to complete various activities to solve the challenge at the end of the unit. Thus, the design challenge can be considered as both an assessment but also an instructional activity. The combination of specific learning targets, meaningful instructional activities, and assessments that closely align with instructional activities provides rich and engaging learning experiences for students and enhances deep learning from multiple disciplines.

The remaining of this chapter provides information about the development of two units that are presented in chapter 4. The first backward map is for the unit that integrates content from ecology and engineering, as well as science and engineering practices (see table 3.1). Briefly, this unit requires students to leverage their content understanding of ecology on a unique design challenge to prototype a two-stage filter for a local water treatment plant. The unit was designed for students to learn about the abiotic and biotic factors that influence ecosystems while simultaneously thinking about the engineering challenge. After being introduced to the challenge in the first lesson and returning to it throughout the unit, students are expected to learn about the various features of ecosystems and then apply their understanding to construct the two-stage water filtration system, with stage 1 being man-made and stage 2 biological in the final lesson. The second backward map is for the unit that integrates science concepts such as cell division and mutations, as well as engineering practices (see table 3.2). The design challenge involves developing a sunscreen formulation that provides effective protection against harmful UV radiation.

TABLE 3.1. *Backward Map for Designing a Two-Stage Water Filter Unit*

DESIRED RESULTS
Established Goals   Through learning about the abiotic and biotic factors that influence ecosystems, students will use their understanding to construct a two-stage water filtration system, with stage 1 being man-made and stage 2 biological.
Standards   *Indiana State Standards in Life Science*   **6.LS2-1** Analyze and interpret data to provide evidence for the effects of resource availability on organisms and populations of organisms in an ecosystem.   **6.LS2-2** Construct an explanation that predicts why patterns of interactions develop between organisms in an ecosystem.   **6.LS2-4** Construct an argument supported by empirical evidence that changes to physical or biological components of an ecosystem affect populations.   *Next Generation Science Standards*   **MS-LS2-1** Analyze and interpret data to provide evidence for the effects of resource availability on organisms and populations of organisms in an ecosystem.   **MS-LS2-4** Construct an argument supported by empirical evidence that changes to physical or biological components of an ecosystem affect populations.   **MS-ETS1-1** Define the criteria and constraints of a design problem with sufficient precision to ensure a successful solution, taking into account relevant scientific principles and potential impacts on people and the natural environment that may limit possible solutions.   **MS-ETS1-2** Evaluate competing design solutions using a systematic process to determine how well they meet the criteria and constraints of the problem.   **MS-ETS1-3** Analyze data from tests to determine similarities and differences among several design solutions to identify the best characteristics of each that can be combined into a new solution to better meet the criteria for success.   **MS-ETS1-4** Develop a model to generate data for iterative testing and modification of a proposed object, tool, or process such that an optimal design can be achieved.

Data Used
Pre- and posttest
Student notebooks
Observations

Understandings	Essential Questions
Students will understand that . . .	1. What are the factors that affect ecosystems?
1. There are biotic and abiotic components to ecosystems that affect the habitat.	2. What are the relationships between various organisms in an ecosystem?
2. Organisms in a given ecosystem exist together in symbiotic relationships.	3. What are examples of symbiotic relationships?
3. Matter is cycled throughout an ecosystem (i.e., water cycle).	4. How does matter move through the ecosystem?
4. Decomposers play a critical role in nutrient cycling in the ecosystem.	5. How does changing the biotic and abiotic factors affect the ecosystem?
5. Changes to biotic or abiotic factors have large effects on ecosystems.	6. What is water filtration?
6. Filtration is a critical process for the health of a particular habitat.	7. What are ways in which water is filtered in nature?
By the end of this unit students will know . . .	By the end of this unit students will be able to . . .
1. Examples of biotic and abiotic factors of ecosystems.	1. Analyze and interpret the organized data to make predictions based on evidence of causal relationships between resource availability, organisms, and organism populations.
2. Abiotic and biotic factors are used in filtration.	2. Make a claim about a given explanation or model for a phenomenon. In their claim, students include the idea that changes to physical or biological components of an ecosystem can affect the populations living there.
3. Examples of various symbiotic relationships and their importance to a functioning ecosystem.	
4. Changes to aspects of an ecosystem or habitat cause specific effects on organisms.	3. Use the model to describe the cycling of matter and flow of energy among living and nonliving parts of the defined system.
5. Water is cycled throughout an ecosystem.	

ASSESSMENT

Performance tasks: Two-stage water filter: stage 1 man-made, stage 2 biological
Self-assessments: Journaling in science notebooks; entrance and exit tickets
Standard assessment: Pre- and posttest

LEARNING PLAN

Lesson 1: Introduction to the Challenge (2 days)

Objective: Students will be able to describe how biotic and abiotic components are used in filtration.
- Review design process and engineering
- Framing the problem using client letters

Lesson 2: Water Cycle and Soil Percolation (2 days)

Objective: Students will be able to describe how abiotic factors affect a habitat.

- Water cycle overview
- Entrance/exit ticket
- Soil percolation lab
- Homework assignment: Written reflection

Lesson 3: What Plants Need to Live (2 days)

Objective: Students will measure and analyze how living things use abiotic factors.

- Plant needs virtual lab
- Transpiration in a plant activity
- Coloring and labeling the internal parts of a plant
- Homework assignment: Research on how plants remove pollution

Lesson 4: Interactions in the Ecosystem (2 days)

Objective: Students will be able to identify the relationship between various organisms.

- Decomposition stations
- Exit ticket reflection
- Good/bad buddies activity
- Oh Deer!

Lesson 5: Create a Two-Stage Filter (5 days)

Objective: Students will be able to construct a two-stage water filtration system, with stage 1 being man-made and stage 2 biological.

- Group brainstorming (groups of 4)
- Split into two groups

Group 1

- Draw design for filter
- Build filter
- Test filter
- Redesign
- Build
- Retest

Group 2

- Research components for ecosystem
- Food web diagram
- Draw the ecosystem

Both groups

- Create a presentation as a whole group
- Present to the class

VOCABULARY

Lesson 1

Constraint
Criteria
Engineer
Engineering
Engineering design process

Lesson 2

Clay
Condensation
Evaporation
Filtration
Groundwater
Percolation
Precipitation
Runoff
Sand
Silt
Transpiration

Lesson 3

Capillary action
Nutrients
Phloem
Xylem

Lesson 4

Abiotic
Biotic
Commensalism
Consumer
Decomposition
Ecosystem
Host
Mutualism
Parasite
Parasitism
Predator
Prey
Producer
Symbiotic relationships

Lesson 5

Abiotic
Biotic
Carnivore
Decomposer
Food web
Herbivore

UNIT CONTEXT AND THE DESIGN CHALLENGE

This unit requires students to leverage their content understanding of ecology on a unique design challenge to prototype a two-stage filter for a local water treatment plant. The design challenge begins with the students working in small groups to determine how to connect the stage 1 filter to stage 2 and how to direct the clean water to the river. After sketching the basic configuration of their filtration system, each group is split into two subgroups—one working on the mechanical filter while the other works on the biological filter. The stage 1 groups focus on the mechanical filtration component of the system. They use household items to design, build, and test a water filtration device. The stage 2 groups focus on the biological component of the filtration system. They research organisms for the ecosystem and create a detailed diagram of this component. The lesson concludes with each group presenting their stage 1 and stage 2 water filters to the class.

TABLE 3.2. *Backward Map for Designing Sunscreen Unit*

DESIRED RESULTS	
Established Goals Through learning about the cell cycle and the mutations that can occur during the cell cycle, students will understand how these errors can lead to cancer. **Standards** *Indiana State Standards in Life Science* **7.LS1-2** Develop and use a model to describe the function of a cell as a whole and ways parts of cells contribute to the function. *Next Generation Science Standards* **MS-LS1-1** Conduct an investigation to provide evidence that living things are made of cells; either one cell or many different numbers and types of cells. **MS-LS1-5** Construct a scientific explanation based on evidence for how environmental and genetic factors influence the growth of organisms. **MS-ETS1-1** Define the criteria and constraints of a design problem with sufficient precision to ensure a successful solution, taking into account relevant scientific principles and potential impacts on people and the natural environment that may limit possible solutions. **MS-ETS1-2** Evaluate competing design solutions using a systematic process to determine how well they meet the criteria and constraints of the problem. **MS-ETS1-3** Analyze data from tests to determine similarities and differences among several design solutions to identify the best characteristics of each that can be combined into a new solution to better meet the criteria for success. **MS-ETS1-4** Develop a model to generate data for iterative testing and modification of a proposed object, tool, or process such that an optimal design can be achieved.	
Data Used Pre- and posttest Student notebooks Observations	
Understandings Students will understand that . . . 1. Cells of multicellular organisms go through the cell cycle to grow, repair, and replace old, damaged, and dying cells. 2. The cell cycle is made up of the phases interphase, mitosis, and cytokinesis, where mitosis is the division of the nucleus and cytokinesis is the division of the cytoplasm. 3. Interphase is made up of G1, S, and G2. 4. Mitosis is made up of the phases prophase, metaphase, anaphase, and telophase. 5. There are various checkpoints during the cell cycle that allow a cell to proceed onward to division. 6. Mutations to the DNA of cells can affect the cells' ability to regulate the cell cycle.	**Essential Questions** 1. What is the cell cycle? 2. What are the phases of the cell cycle? 3. What is mitosis? 4. What are the phases of mitosis? 5. How is the cell cycle regulated? 6. What is cancer? 7. How are the cell cycle and mitosis related to cancer?

7. Cancer is the uncontrolled growth of cells. 8. The cell cycle and cancer are interrelated because unregulated cell growth leads to cancer.	
By the end of this unit students will know . . . 1. Cells go through the cell cycle to grow, repair, and replace damaged cells in multicellular organisms. 2. The cell cycle consists of stages that are moderated by various checkpoints. 3. Cancer is uncontrolled cell growth. 4. Cancer has many causes, one of which is damage to DNA by UVA and UVB rays.	By the end of this unit students will be able to . . . 1. Create a model of the cell cycle. 2. Modify that model to reflect controls on cell division. 3. Develop an effective sunscreen formula. 4. Create a persuasive presentation.

ASSESSMENT

Performance tasks: Cell cycle model; sunscreen formula development
Self-assessments: Journaling in science notebooks; KWPL (what I *know*, what I *want* to know, what I *predict*, what I *learned*)
Standard assessment: Pre- and posttest

LEARNING PLAN

Lesson 1: Introduction to the Challenge (1 day)

Objective: Students will be able to identify the engineering problem and break it down into the important components.

- Students identify the scope of the problem and need-to-knows.

Lesson 2: Cell Division (3 days)

Objectives: Students will be able to identify and define the stages of the cell cycle: interphase, prophase, metaphase, anaphase, telophase, and cytokinesis. Students will be able to describe what is happening in each phase. Students will be able to create a model of the cell cycle to explain how the cells in multicellular organisms repeatedly divide to make more cells for growth and repair.

- Stations activities (Stations will introduce students to the salient details of the cell cycle without the need for teachers to lecture.)
- Model activity (string, animation, whiteboards, flip-books, etc.)

Lesson 3: What Causes Cancer (3 days)

Objectives: Students will be able to understand the importance of the checkpoints in mitosis. Students will be able to explain how mutations in cells can lead to cancer.

- Reading about checkpoints of the cell cycle
- Add checkpoints to model of cell cycle
- Mitotic index lab

Lesson 4: Creation of Sunscreen (5 days)

Objective: Students will be able to create an effective formula for sunscreen that prevents UVA and UVB rays from harming cells.

- Sunscreen formula creation
- Sunscreen testing

Lesson 5: Shark Tank (3–4 days)

Objective: Students will share out their formulas and the results of testing during a Shark Tank–style presentation.
- Determine cost of sunscreen
- Practice presentations
- Presentations
- Post-unit test

VOCABULARY	
Lesson 1 Constraint Criteria Engineer Engineering Engineering design process **Lesson 2** Anaphase Cytokinesis Cytoplasm Interphase Metaphase Nucleus Prophase Telophase	**Lesson 3** Cell checkpoints G_1 phase G_2 phase Growth hormone Metastasize S phase **Lesson 4** Castor oil Shea butter UV beads Zinc oxide **Lesson 5** N/A

UNIT CONTEXT AND THE DESIGN CHALLENGE

Students receive a memo from a hypothetical client who is asking for their help to design a safe and effective sunscreen formula. After learning about cell cycle, mutations, and cancer, students test various ingredients to design their sunscreen formula. They identify four ingredients they think are most important in a sunscreen and identify the reasons for their decision. They then test the effectiveness of their sunscreen formula and present their design in Shark Tank format.

4

SAMPLE CURRICULUM UNITS

This chapter presents several lessons from two curriculum units: Designing a Two-Stage Water Filter and Designing Sunscreen. Both units were field-tested and address Indiana Science Education Standards and the Next Generation Science Standards. In brief, the first unit, Designing a Two-Stage Water Filter (tables 4.1–4.6), includes five lessons. After being introduced to the challenge in the first lesson and returning to it throughout the unit, students are expected to learn about the various features of ecosystems and then apply their understanding to construct the two-stage water filtration system, with stage 1 being man-made and stage 2 biological in the final lesson. The second unit, Designing Sunscreen (tables 4.7–4.14), provides students unique learning activities to explore cell cycle, mutations, and cancer while designing sunscreen. This unit also includes five lessons. The design challenge is introduced in the first lesson, and students complete the design challenge in lessons four and five after learning about the relevant science concepts.

Designing a Two-Stage Water Filter

BY VALARIE BOGAN, SHELBI SMEATHERS, AND S. SELCEN GUZEY

UNIT OVERVIEW

GRADE LEVEL: 6th grade

APPROXIMATE TIME NEEDED TO COMPLETE UNIT: 13 class periods (650 minutes)

UNIT SUMMARY:
Through learning about the abiotic and biotic factors that influence ecosystems, students will use their understanding to construct a two-stage water filtration system, with stage 1 being man-made and stage 2 biological.

STANDARDS ADDRESSED
INDIANA STATE STANDARDS IN LIFE SCIENCE

- **6.LS2-1** Analyze and interpret data to provide evidence for the effects of resource availability on organisms and populations of organisms in an ecosystem.
- **6.LS2-2** Construct an explanation that predicts why patterns of interactions develop between organisms in an ecosystem.
- **6.LS2-4** Construct an argument supported by empirical evidence that changes to physical or biological components of an ecosystem affect populations.

NEXT GENERATION SCIENCE STANDARDS

- **MS-LS2-1** Analyze and interpret data to provide evidence for the effects of resource availability on organisms and populations of organisms in an ecosystem.
- **MS-LS2-4** Construct an argument supported by empirical evidence that changes to physical or biological components of an ecosystem affect populations.
- **MS-ETS1-1** Define the criteria and constraints of a design problem with sufficient precision to ensure a successful solution, taking into account relevant scientific principles and potential impacts on people and the natural environment that may limit possible solutions.
- **MS-ETS1-2** Evaluate competing design solutions using a systematic process to determine how well they meet the criteria and constraints of the problem.
- **MS-ETS1-3** Analyze data from tests to determine similarities and differences among several design solutions to identify the best characteristics of each that can be combined into a new solution to better meet the criteria for success.
- **MS-ETS1-4** Develop a model to generate data for iterative testing and modification of a proposed object, tool, or process such that an optimal design can be achieved.

LESSONS

    Lesson 1: Introduction to the Challenge
    Lesson 2: Water Cycle and Soil Percolation
    Lesson 3: What Plants Need to Live
    Lesson 4: Interactions in the Ecosystem
    Lesson 5: Creating the Two-Stage Filtration System

SAMPLE LESSON PLANS (LESSONS 1, 2, AND 5)

TABLE 4.1. *Designing a Two-Stage Water Filter Unit, Lesson 1*

LESSON 1	INTRODUCTION TO THE CHALLENGE
TIME REQUIRED	**LESSON SUMMARY**
100 min. (2 × 50-min. class periods)	The lesson is an introduction to the engineering design process, the engineering challenge, and overall problem framing. Students will engage in discussion to frame the problem and use the client letter to set up the next steps of the unit.
STANDARDS ADDRESSED	
\multicolumn{2}{l}{**Next Generation Science Standards**}
\multicolumn{2}{l}{**MS-ETS1-1** Define the criteria and constraints of a design problem with sufficient precision to ensure a successful solution, taking into account relevant scientific principles and potential impacts on people and the natural environment that may limit possible solutions.}
VOCABULARY	**OBJECTIVES**
Constraint Criteria Engineer Engineering Engineering design process	By the end of the lesson, students will • Understand what engineers do through discussion. • Learn the steps of the design process through review discussion. • Outline the design challenge and problem from the client during the lesson. By the end of the lesson, students will know • An engineer is a person who designs solutions to problems. • Engineering design is an iterative process of development, testing, and improvement. • Ecosystems depend on the filtration and cycling of water.
SAFETY CONSIDERATIONS	
\multicolumn{2}{l}{N/A}
BEFORE THE LESSON	
\multicolumn{2}{l}{1. Copy the design process page (see figure 4.1). 2. Copy the client letter (see below). 3. Copy the student Problem Scoping Worksheet (see below).}

ASSESSMENTS	CLASSROOM INSTRUCTIONS
PRE-ACTIVITY ASSESSMENT	**INTRODUCTION**

N/A	Introduce the Unit
	Say: This unit is about water pollution. You will construct a two-stage water filtration system, with stage 1 being man-made and stage 2 biological, to help solve a water pollution problem in the city of Willow Creek.
	  Learn from Students
	Ask: What does water pollution mean?
	  Do we experience water pollution in our city?
	  Who could solve the water pollution–related problems we have in our city?

ACTIVITY EMBEDDED ASSESSMENT	**ACTIVITIES**

Listen to student responses throughout individual and class discussion.	Review Design Process
	Say: Several types of engineers work on water pollution problems. What types of engineers do you think focus on controlling water pollution or improving water quality? OK, let's step back and talk about engineers. What do engineers do? What kinds of engineers are there? What steps do engineers take to accomplish a goal and design a product? *Allow students to respond and share.*
	Discuss: Review design phone image (figure 4.1) with students.
	  Identify Problem (Information Gathering)
	  Share Letter from Client.
	Say: Now you are going to act as engineers to frame the problem in small groups (no larger than four). *Allow students time to work to frame the problem using the worksheet. They will need more information to complete all of the questions, so when students reach a natural break share Letter from Client (below).*
	• *Who is the client?*
	• *What is the problem?*
	• *What is the client asking for?*
	• *Who are the end-users?*
	• *What are the requirements (criteria) and limitations (constraints)?*
	Come back together as a whole group to discuss and collect responses to come to consensus as a class (information gathering).
	Lead discussion as a class: *It is critical that students are encouraged to share many perspectives on the problem. You should encourage them to think differently about each question.*
	Ask: Who did you identify as the client?
	  City?
	  Consumers?
	  Wastewater treatment people?
	Ask: What is the problem?
	  Clean water?
	  Fish kills?
	  Human health?
	  Environmental health?
	  Rain?

	Ask: What is the client asking for? Water filter device?
	Ask: Who are the end-users? Humans? Animals/fish in the ecosystem?
	Ask: What are the requirements (criteria) and limitations (constraints)?
POST-ACTIVITY ASSESSMENT	**CLOSURE**
N/A	Review steps of design process achieved so far, and prep for moving on to digging deeper in subsequent classes. **Say:** So far, where are we in the design process? *Allow students to respond. Students should identify the EXPLOREit phase.* **Say:** Tomorrow, we will dig deeper and take a look at some of the content pieces the client asked that we discuss. **Ask:** What did the client say we will need to be learning? *Refer students to section of client letter where client discusses what teacher needs to teach students.*

CLIENT LETTER

City of Willow Creek
Dave Smith
Environmental Engineer
500 S. University St.
Willow Creek, IN 47407

Dear Students:

We are writing you to provide specific information about the water pollution problem we have in our local creek. When it rains, water from streets and sidewalks flows into storm drains. We have a system that filters stormwater before going into our creek. However, in the last few years, we noticed that during heavy rain, our system doesn't work properly. Thus, the collected stormwater goes straight into our creek before being properly filtered.

Now, we need your help! The City of Willow Creek Engineering Office is asking each student engineering team to design a better filter for the stormwater pipe. Specifically, the engineering office would like the students to create a two-stage filter. The first stage will be mechanical, and the secondary filter will be biological. The engineering team's designs will be constrained by material, time, quality of filtration, and flow rates. The teams will create a filter for a round 4-foot pipe. The filter will be a scale model of what would go inside the pipe. The water should be safe to enter the river after exiting the filter, and the filter should not cause a backup in the system.

Your team will create a report that explains the problem, shows your science experiments and data, includes sketches of your design, and shares the results of your tests. The report should include a justification for the design. Students must provide data to support their decision to create the prototype as per their team's design.

To help you get ready for this important task, your teacher will guide you in learning about soil percolation, the water cycle, plant needs, and ecosystem interactions.

It is important that you use the design process and document all findings. Our engineering team will use your reports to help decide what kind of filter to build.

We're excited to see your creative solutions!

Sincerely,
Dave Smith

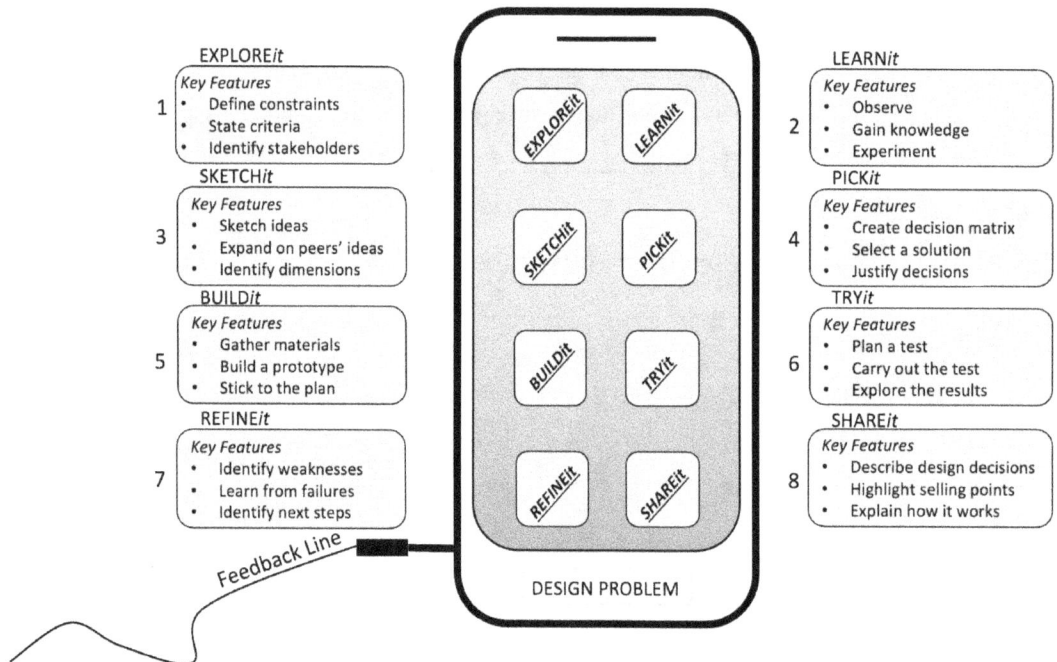

FIGURE 4.1. Design phone for engineering design process.

PROBLEM SCOPING WORKSHEET
WHAT? HOW? WHY?

DIRECTIONS: With your group, construct a response to each of the following questions.

1. Who is the client?

2. What is the client's problem that needs a solution? Be certain to explain why this problem is important to solve. Use information from the client to support your reasons.

3. Who are the end users?

4. What will make the solution effective (criteria)? Use detailed information from the client.

5. What will limit how you can solve the problem (constraints)? Use detailed information you have from the client.

6. What did the client say you need to learn, and your teacher needs to teach you about, in order to solve this problem?

TABLE 4.2. *Designing a Two-Stage Water Filter Unit, Lesson 2*

LESSON 2	WATER CYCLE AND SOIL PERCOLATION
TIME REQUIRED	LESSON SUMMARY
100 min. (2 × 50-min. class periods)	This lesson connects to students' previous activities with their framing of the problem. During the lesson, students will better understand how water is moved throughout an ecosystem (water cycling) and how soil types affect the percolation of water.
STANDARDS ADDRESSED	
Indiana State Standards in Life Science **6.LS2-1** Analyze and interpret data to provide evidence for the effects of resource availability on organisms and populations of organisms in an ecosystem. **6.LS2-4** Construct an argument supported by empirical evidence that changes to physical or biological components of an ecosystem affect populations. **Next Generation Science Standards** **MS-LS2-1** Analyze and interpret data to provide evidence for the effects of resource availability on organisms and populations of organisms in an ecosystem. **MS-LS2-4** Construct an argument supported by empirical evidence that changes to physical or biological components of an ecosystem affect populations.	
VOCABULARY	OBJECTIVES
Clay Condensation Evaporation Filtration Groundwater	During the lesson, students will • Understand the importance of percolation of water in the water cycle through discussion. • Describe and build a model for how matter (water) is cycled through the ecosystem after soil percolation and water cycle activity.

Percolation Precipitation Runoff Sand Silt Transpiration	• Model how different substances affect the percolation of water during soil percolation activity. • Discuss how the availability of water and the components of soil affect populations in an ecosystem through reflection after soil percolation activity. By the end of the lesson, students will know • Soil is composed of many different substances, including sand, silt, and clay. • Soil is considered an abiotic factor of the environment. • The amounts of the different particles in soil (sand, silt, or clay) affect the percolation of water and the runoff of the water. • Percolation is the straining of water through a filter, either natural or man-made.

MATERIALS

Per Class

30 large clear plastic cups
2–3 lb. of dirt
2–3 lb. of sand
2–3 lb. of gravel
Thumbtack to punch holes in cup
Water
8–10 × 100 mL graduated cylinders
8–10 × 250 mL beakers
Funnels and measuring cups
Spoons (optional)
Balances (optional)

Per Group

2 plastic cups (1 with holes, 1 for pouring water)
Water
1 funnel
1 × 100 mL graduated cylinder
1 × 250 mL beaker

SAFETY CONSIDERATIONS

Monitor students during use of glassware. Have appropriate site for disposal of broken glass available in classroom in case of accident.

BEFORE THE LESSON

1. Familiarize yourself with Soil Percolation Lab activity structure.
2. Give students access to Soil Percolation Student Worksheet (see below).
3. Prepare soil percolation materials.
4. Prepare model of soil percolation system for demo.
5. Give students access to exit/entrance ticket (see below).
6. Give students access to Student Reflection prompt (see below).

SAMPLE CURRICULUM UNITS / 23

ASSESSMENTS	CLASSROOM INSTRUCTIONS
PRE-ACTIVITY ASSESSMENT	**INTRODUCTION**
Listen to student responses. Prompt students to recall all the facts about water and water treatment.	Activate Prior Knowledge **Say:** Yesterday, we read the client letter. Who can remember some of the facts we learned in the letter about water and water treatment? *Allow students to respond.* Refer to Design Process **Ask:** Where are we in the design process? *Students should identify the LEARNit phase.*
ACTIVITY EMBEDDED ASSESSMENT	**ACTIVITIES**
Circulate around the room. As students are reading and completing drawings, circulate around the room, checking for student understanding.	**INTRODUCE THE WATER CYCLE (DAY 1)** **Say:** So now, we are going to try to address some of these things with a few activities over the next few days. Together we are going to talk about water. **Ask:** Where do we see water in nature? Where does water come from? How does it get into lakes, rivers, streams? *Encourage students to think about how water gets into their homes and how water moves through ecosystems in a cycle.* *As students come up with ideas, ask them to draw a picture.* **Say:** Now, together, we are going to organize these ideas in a more detailed picture. *Hand out blank pieces of paper, or have students use their digital notebooks if you would like them to turn this in.* Together, let's draw a picture of the water cycle. I will help you get started. Remember that a cycle has no beginning or end, so let's start with water in the atmosphere as condensation. To represent this, you might draw a cloud. *On the board, draw a cloud and add the word "condensation."* **Ask:** Where does water go from here? How does water get from clouds to the ground? **Instruct:** Lead students in discussion of words and add definitions associated with the water cycle to a running list on the board. • Condensation • Precipitation • Runoff • Percolation • Transpiration • Evaporation • Groundwater *Give students 5–10 minutes to complete their pictures, interjecting to help students to may get stuck. Prompt them with questions and add to your picture on the board.*
Check for understanding with exit ticket or entrance ticket. Have students fill in terms on a picture of the water cycle as they leave/enter the class.	**Natural break:** If necessary, this is a natural break in this lesson. Before students leave for the day, have them fill out the exit ticket. If short on time, you could amend this to be an entrance ticket for the following day.

Circulate around the room. As students are working in groups, circulate around the room. Be certain to check in with students who had incorrect responses on the exit/entrance ticket. See Assessments Continued section below.

Complete Soil Percolation Lab (Day 2)

Detailed lab instructions are provided below.

Notes about instructions: This lab will be completed in a jigsaw manner where different groups of students will work to answer one specific question, then groups will collaborate by putting their answers on the board to answer all questions together. The three questions students will be investigating reflect the variables involved in the soil percolation model (sand, soil, and gravel). The initial teacher demonstration is modeling of two controls: one control with all three materials in equal distribution; the other control with no material, allowing all of the water to flow through the cup.

Instructions

Say: Yesterday, we looked at the water cycle. One of the most important features of the water cycle is the filtration or percolation of water through the soil into the ground. *Explain how water gets into aquifers or to a river or lake, and how humans draw upon this water using wells or pumps.*

Ask: So, who has been outside shortly after it rains or precipitates? What do you notice about where the water is going? *Listen to student responses. Students should note flooding.*

Demonstration of Controls for Students

Explain to students: They are going to examine variables that affect the ability of water to soak, percolate, or filter into the ground. On this table, they have different materials that are all found in soil. *Explain the different materials to students. Be certain to ask if they have seen or heard about these materials.*

With their groups, they will design and carry out a test to see how the different materials affect the amount of water that can get through the system, and the class will all collaborate to understand how all of these materials work together to determine the filtration of water. At this point, demonstrate the model for students. *Explain model that you created to students and the amounts of the materials that you used. Then, after 1 minute, pour water through model and measure the amount of water that flows out of the system using the graduated cylinder. Additionally, explain the use of the control cup with no materials. Add the amount of water that flowed through your system to the board under the heading Control 1. Do the same for Control 2.*

Allow Students to Design

Break students into groups: Students should be in groups of preferably no more than three. If necessary, groups of four are OK, but encourage students to define roles (e.g., materials collector, scribe, timekeeper, measuring expert, etc.).

Instruct: Explain to groups that each group will be assigned to test one of the materials for its effect on filtration and they will add their conclusions to the board. At this point, assign each group either sand, soil, or gravel. There should be duplicate or triplicate groups investigating each material. *Write the three words "sand," "soil," and "gravel" or the questions below on the board so students can add their conclusions and observations.*

1. How does the amount of <u>sand</u> affect the filtration of water?
2. How does the amount of <u>dirt</u> affect the filtration of water?
3. How does the amount of <u>gravel</u> affect the filtration of water?

Assign design: Give groups the Soil Percolation Student Worksheet (see below) and assign them to design their experiment, specifically what materials and in what amount will go into their cups. Inform them that they will all start with the same amount of water (100 mL) to add to their system and must measure the amount of water collected in the beaker after exactly 1 minute. Additionally, they must use the same total volume of materials that you used. For example, if you used exactly 1 cup (⅓ gravel, ⅓ dirt, ⅓ sand), their materials must also total 1 cup although, in different ratios (e.g., the sand group might have ½ cup sand, ¼ dirt, ¼ gravel; 1 cup sand only; ⅔ sand, ⅙ dirt, ⅙ gravel).

Give students appropriate time to design. Circulate around the room for questions.

Prompt the students to discuss the following questions:

1. What materials is your group going to choose?
2. Why are you choosing these materials?
3. What do you think will happen when you run your tests? Do you think a lot of water or a little bit of water will come through? Why do you think this?

Check students' designs to make sure their experiments are not confounded— that they are only measuring the effect of the material you assigned them, all of their materials add up to the same total volume used in your demonstration (although in a different ratio), they plan on using 100 mL of water, and they are testing for 1 minute.

Testing

After you have approved their design, give students time to run one or two tests of their design.

While students are testing, ask the following questions for each group to discuss:

- What do you notice about the water at the start versus the water at the end?
- Where do you have runoff in your system? What is runoff?
- Where do you have percolation in your system? What is percolation?
- Do you have filtration in your system? What is filtration?
- How is percolation different from filtration?

Have students write the total amount of water they had at the end of their design and one observation about what happened during their experiment on the board under their respective Control 1 and Control 2 headings.

Debrief

With students, discuss the overall findings of the class. If time allows, you might have all the students who tested each respective material gather together to come up with a summary statement of their findings that they can share out to the class. Additionally, as time allows, you could have them reconfigure into groups in which each member tested a different material and compare and contrast their findings. Ultimately students should understand that different materials affect the filtration of water in different ways.

	Tips for Running Discussion
	Because of the nature of this lab, students might have a difficult time understanding/making sense of the data they collected. Not all students will have used the same method to test their respective variable (or isolated their variable), and while that is fine, they might note this as a challenge for making sense of the data. Use the following questions/techniques to guide the discussion. 1. What trends do you notice from the data about the sand/soil/gravel? 2. Can we calculate a flow rate for each variable? 3. How does each material affect the flow rate of water? 4. Draw students' attention to the natural layers or mixing of these variables in soil in nature. How might this affect the flow of water? 5. In what circumstances would we find more sandy soil? More gravel in soil? 6. If you were designing an ecosystem to accommodate a large rain/water event, what type of soil would you want?
POST-ACTIVITY ASSESSMENT	**CLOSURE**
Student reflection assignment	After students finish the lab activity, ask them to complete a reflection assignment for homework (see below). **Say:** Tonight for homework, I would like for you to write a paragraph (3–5 sentences) answering the following questions. *(Write questions on the board and have students access questions in digital notebooks to turn in to you.)* 1. How did the materials we used in our design affect the amount of water that flowed through the system? 2. How do you think the availability of water might affect the living things in an ecosystem?
ASSESSMENTS CONTINUED	
During the lesson and activities, it will be important to prompt students with questions to determine how they are thinking. Following are examples of these questions. • What are examples of precipitation? • Where does runoff water go? • How does this relate to the design challenge from the wastewater treatment plant? During the lab activity: • What materials did you choose? • Why did you choose these materials? • What do you think will happen? Do you think a lot of water or a little bit of water will come through? Why do you think this? • What do you notice about the water at the start versus the water at the end? • Where do you have runoff in your system? What is runoff? • Where do you have percolation in your system? What is percolation? • Do you have filtration in your system? What is filtration? • How is percolation different from filtration? • How does this relate to the design challenge from the wastewater treatment plant? • Do you think the availability of water affects living things? What might happen to living things if no water is available at the end of your system? What might happen if there is a lot of water available?	

SOIL PERCOLATION LAB
TEACHER INSTRUCTIONS

OBJECTIVE: Students will model how different substances affect the percolation of water during soil percolation activity.

MATERIALS

    Clear plastic cups (2 per student group)
    Thumbtack for punching holes in plastic cups
    Sand
    Dirt/soil
    Gravel
    Water or access to sink
    Measuring cups
    250 mL beakers (1 per student group)
    100 mL graduated cylinder (1 per student group)
    Spoons
    Balances

THE SETUP

Prior to class, complete the following items:

1. Punch three holes in the bottom of one cup for each student group. (The other cup does not need holes and will be used to pour water into their experimental setup.)
2. Put out sand, soil, and gravel with measuring cups or spoons and balances so students can easily procure specific amounts of each material for their own experimental setup.
3. Create your demonstration cup (Control 1).
    a. Punch holes in cup.
    b. Load with layer of gravel, soil, and sand in equal parts.
4. Prepare Control 2 by punching holes in another cup.

NOTES ABOUT INSTRUCTION

This lab will be completed in a jigsaw manner where different groups of students will work to answer one specific question, then groups will collaborate by putting their answers on the board to answer all questions together. The three questions students will be investigating reflect the variables involved in the soil percolation model (sand, soil, and gravel). The initial teacher demonstration is modeling of two controls: one control with all three materials in equal distribution; the other control with no material, allowing all of the water to flow through the cup.

INSTRUCTIONS

1. DEMONSTRATION OF CONTROLS FOR STUDENTS

Explain to students: They are going to examine variables that affect the ability of water to soak, percolate, or filter into the ground. On this table, they have different materials that are all found in soil. *Explain the different materials to students. Be certain to ask if they have seen or heard about these materials.*

With their groups, they will design and carry out a test to see how the different materials affect the amount of water that can get through the system, and the class will all collaborate to understand how all of these materials work together to determine the filtration of water. At this point, demonstrate the model for students. *Explain model that you created to students and the amounts of the materials that you used. Then, after 1 minute, pour water through model and measure the amount of water that flows out of the system using the graduated cylinder. Additionally, explain the use of the control cup with no materials. Add the amount of water that flowed through your system to the board under the heading Control 1. Do the same for Control 2.*

2. ALLOW STUDENTS TO DESIGN

Break students into groups: Students should be in groups of preferably no more than three. If necessary, groups of four are OK, but encourage students to define roles (e.g., materials collector, scribe, timekeeper, measuring expert, etc.).

Instruct: Explain to groups that each group will be assigned to test one of the materials for its effect on filtration and they will add their conclusions to the board. At this point, assign each group either sand, soil, or gravel. There should be duplicate or triplicate groups investigating each material. *Write the three words "sand," "soil," and "gravel" or the questions below on the board so students can add their conclusions and observations.*

1. How does the amount of <u>sand</u> affect the filtration of water?
2. How does the amount of <u>dirt</u> affect the filtration of water?
3. How does the amount of <u>gravel</u> affect the filtration of water?

Assign design: Give groups the Soil Percolation Student Worksheet (see below) and assign them to design their experiment, specifically what materials and in what amount will go into their cups. Inform them that they will all start with the same amount of water (100 mL) to add to their system and must measure the amount of water collected in the beaker after exactly 1 minute. Additionally, they must use the same total volume of materials that you used. For example, if you used exactly 1 cup (⅓ gravel, ⅓ dirt, ⅓ sand) their materials must also total 1 cup, although in different ratios (e.g., the sand group might have ½ cup sand, ¼ dirt, ¼ gravel; 1 cup sand only; ⅔ sand, ⅙ dirt, ⅙ gravel).

Give students appropriate time to design. Circulate around the room for questions.

Prompt the students to discuss the following questions:

1. What materials is your group going to choose?
2. Why are you choosing these materials?
3. What do you think will happen when you run your tests? Do you think a lot of water or a little bit of water will come through? Why do you think this?

Check students' designs to make sure their experiments are not confounded—that they are only measuring the effect of the material you assigned them, all of their materials add up to the same total volume used in your demonstration (although in a different ratio), they plan on using 100 mL of water, and they are testing for 1 minute.

3. TESTING

After you have approved their design, give students time to run one or two tests of their design.

While students are testing, ask the following questions for each group to discuss:

- What do you notice about the water at the start versus the water at the end?
- Where do you have runoff in your system? What is runoff?
- Where do you have percolation in your system? What is percolation?
- Do you have filtration in your system? What is filtration?
- How is percolation different from filtration?

Have students write the total amount of water they had at the end of their design and one observation about what happened during their experiment on the board under their respective Control 1 and Control 2 headings.

4. DEBRIEF AND CLOSURE

Debrief: With students, discuss the overall findings of the class. If time allows, you might have all the students who tested each respective material gather together to come up with a summary statement of their findings that they can share out to the class. Additionally, as time allows, you could have them reconfigure into groups in which each member tested a different material and compare and contrast their findings. Ultimately students should understand that different materials affect the filtration of water in different ways.

Closure: Refer to the closure activity in lesson plan. Say:

> Tonight for homework, I would like for you to write a paragraph (3–5 sentences) answering the following questions. (Write questions on the board and have students access questions in digital notebooks to turn in to you.) (1) How did the materials we used in our design affect the amount of water that flowed through the system? (2) How do you think the availability of water might affect the living things in an ecosystem?

SOIL PERCOLATION LAB
STUDENT WORKSHEET

Names of Group Members: _____

DIRECTIONS: With your group you are going to examine one of the variables that affect the ability of water to soak, percolate, or filter through soil. This is important because soil can act as a natural filter, and if you are to design a filter for the water treatment plant, you need to consider what types of soil, and how much of each type, you should include in your design.

UNDERSTAND THE CONTROLS

DIRECTIONS: Below, draw the cups with the amounts of each material your teacher had in their cups during their demonstration. Then add the amount of water that flowed through the cups into the graduated cylinder after 60 seconds.

Which cup had the most water flow out of it? _____
Why do you think this happened? _____
Which cup had the least water flow out of it? _____
Why do you think this happened? _____

DESIGN YOUR EXPERIMENT

DIRECTIONS: Now with your group, you are going to dig deeper into understanding the three materials (soil, sand, and gravel) and how they each affect the filtration of water. Your teacher will assign a material for you to test.

REMEMBER! It is important to design a test where you are certain you are only testing <u>one variable at a time</u>! If you change the amount of two or more materials, you may not be designing a good test.

Material we were assigned to test: Sand   Soil   Gravel
(Circle one)

OUR DESIGN
We are going to fill our cup with: _____
We chose these materials because _____

Drawing of materials in our cup:

DESIGN CHOICES TO MAKE

1. How much water are we going to start with?

2. How long will we allow the water to run through the system?

3. How many times are we going to run our test?

4. Are we going to run it the same way each time?

5. How can we chart our results and observations to share them with the class?

Teacher signature of approval before we test: _____

RESULTS OF OUR TESTS

DIRECTIONS: Record your results and observations below.

QUESTIONS TO CONSIDER

1. How did the amount of water at the end of our tests compare with the control demonstration by our teacher?

2. Why was there a difference?

3. How did the material we tested affect the amount of water at the end?

4. If we were to make a filter, would we want to use a lot of our material? Why?

5. If we were to make a filter, would we want to use a little of our material? Why?

Name: _____

STUDENT REFLECTION

DIRECTIONS: Write one paragraph (3–5 sentences) to in response to each of the two questions below.

1. How did the materials we used in our design affect the amount of water that flowed through the system?

2. How do you think the availability of water might affect the living things in an ecosystem?

TABLE 4.3. *Designing a Two-Stage Water Filter Unit, Lesson 5*

LESSON 5	CREATING THE TWO-STAGE FILTRATION SYSTEM
TIME REQUIRED	**LESSON SUMMARY**
250 mins. (5 × 50 min. class periods)	Students will design, build, test, and redesign a two-stage water filtration system, with stage 1 being man-made and stage 2 biological.
STANDARDS ADDRESSED	
Next Generation Science Standards **MS-ETS1-2** Evaluate competing design solutions using a systematic process to determine how well they meet the criteria and constraints of the problem. **MS-ETS1-3** Analyze data from tests to determine similarities and differences among several design solutions to identify the best characteristics of each that can be combined into a new solution to better meet the criteria for success. **MS-ETS1-4** Develop a model to generate data for iterative testing and modification of a proposed object, tool, or process such that an optimal design can be achieved.	
VOCABULARY	**OBJECTIVE**
Abiotic Biotic Carnivore Decomposer Food web Herbivore	Students will construct a two-stage water filtration system, with stage 1 being man-made and stage 2 biological.
MATERIALS	
Per Class Package of 50 coffee filters Large roll paper towels ¼ bag pea gravel ¼ bag sand ¼ bag large gravel ¼ bottle aquarium charcoal 1 bag cotton balls 2 large boxes gauze pads 2 rolls scotch tape 1 roll masking tape	

SAMPLE CURRICULUM UNITS / 33

SAFETY CONSIDERATIONS	
⚠️ **Irritant: It Bothers**	
"These substances can irritate your eyes and skin causing itchiness, soreness, redness and blistering. Don't mistake them for being harmless either, they can also cause toxicity if you swallow them." (Arpita Das, "Safety Comes First: Common Laboratory Signs," last updated March 30, 2023, https://bitesizebio.com/28135/safety-comes-first-common-laboratory-signs/.)	
BEFORE THE LESSON	
N/A	
ASSESSMENTS	**CLASSROOM INSTRUCTIONS**
PRE-ACTIVITY ASSESSMENT	**INTRODUCTION**
N/A	*Day 1*
	Create groups of four by randomly assigning students to groups.
	Say: Today we are going to combine all the knowledge we have gained throughout the unit by starting our engineering project.
	Ask: How many of you remember the letter from our client we received at the beginning of the unit? Can anyone remind us of what was said in the letter about the treatment of stormwater?
	Say: Please read the handout Designing a Filtration System (see below) carefully. *Allow students a couple of minutes to read the handout.*
	Ask: What information from the last few weeks will be helpful in developing these filters?
	Ask: Where are we in the design process? *Students should identify the SKETCHit phase.*
	Say: Before you can start designing the two stages of your filtration system, we need to figure out how the two filters will be connected to each other and how the water will get back to the river after the filtration is finished.
	Ask: How can we get water out of the first-stage filter and into the second? Make sure the students understand that the water will need to exit the stage 1 filter and flow into the stage 2 filter. A lot of possibilities would work, such as a pipe, a hose, or a ditch. *Allow students to share their ideas and come to a consensus as a class.*
	Say: Now that we have created a way for the water to exit the stage 2 filter and enter the river, does anybody have any ideas? *Be sure the students understand the second stage filter is an open area where their plants and animals will live; it is not something that goes inside a pipe. Again, there are many ways the class can decide to move the water from stage 2 into the river: a pipe, a hose, and a ditch. Allow the students to share their ideas and then come to a consensus as a class.*
	Say: Once you have decided how your group will divide into two subgroups, let me know and I will direct you to the correct materials. *Confirm that the groups have completed the rough draft and grouping decisions before handing out the project sheets. The stage 1 groups should be working on material decisions and sketching a rough drawing.*
	The stage 2 groups should be researching ecosystem components.

ACTIVITY EMBEDDED ASSESSMENT	ACTIVITIES
N/A	*Day 2* **Say:** Everyone needs to be working on their assigned task today. This is the first of three project days. Each group needs to be finished within the next three class periods. **Ask:** Before we get started, does anyone have a question for the good of the group? *The stage 1 groups should be completing drawings, getting approval for their design, and starting to build.* *The stage 2 groups should be continuing to research.* *Walk around the room while the students are working. Be sure to visit each group at least once.* **Ask:** For each stage 1 group: Why did you choose these materials? Why did you decide to structure your filter in that way? For each stage 2 group: Are you having any trouble locating the information you need? What organisms have you chosen for your ecosystem? *Days 3–4* **Say:** Everyone needs to be working on their assigned task today. This is the second of three project days. Each group needs to be completely finished within the next two class periods. **Ask:** Before we get started, does anyone have a question for the good of the group? *The stage 1 groups should be completing building, and testing if there is time.* *The stage 2 groups should be starting their drawings.* *Walk around the room while the students are working. Be sure to visit each group at least once.* **Ask:** • For each stage 1 group: What is your flow rate prediction for this design (amount of water/unit of time)? • For each stage 2 group: What producers did you choose for your ecosystem? Why did you make that choice?
POST-ACTIVITY ASSESSMENT	**CLOSURE**
See rubrics for stage 1 and 2 filters.	*Day 5* Group presentations. **Say:** Today, we are going to be presenting all your hard work to the class. During these presentations your best active listening is expected and appreciated. *Allow students to ask questions of each group.* **For each group ask the following:** • What did you learn from doing this project? • Was there anything you feel like we should have studied before making this filter that wasn't covered in the unit?

> **EDUCATOR RESOURCES**
>
> **Teacher Guidelines**
>
> A note on the timing for the stage 1 groups: Not all groups will get to tasks 4–6. It depends on how time-efficient they are and how well they work as a group. It isn't ideal for the groups to just test once, but it is enough to accomplish the learning goals.
>
> In order to reduce the cost of the activity and reduce material waste, you will need to approve each group's design before they start building. Groups are limited to four of the eight materials listed and must justify the choices they make on their project sheet. Be sure to pay attention to the amount of materials written in their design. If it seems excessive, make them reduce their usage and then bring the plan back for a second chance at approval.
>
> Create the testing liquid by filling a washed-out milk jug ¾ of the way full from any outdoor water source—for example a puddle, pond, or stream. If you can't access one of these water sources you may, as a last resort, use tap water. To this add some crushed dead leaves, dirt, small pieces of stick, and some toilet paper. Shake well before each test. To make it abundantly clear that this water is not to be consumed, wear eye protection and disposable gloves when pouring. If possible, have the students wear eye protection, gloves, and lab aprons when testing the stage 1 filter. Have the students start the timers as soon as they start pouring the liquid onto the filter. They will continue timing until the water has flowed through the filter. In the best-case scenario, you should be standing with the group as they do the testing so you can grade the performance while the test is taking place. If you are unable to be with a group, make sure that they know to call you over after the test and before they dispose of the filter. Be sure to have two or three buckets where the students can dispose of their materials. The water that is in the bottom of the beakers should be poured into one of the buckets while the filter materials are disposed of in the other buckets. If you would like to reuse the gravel or aquarium charcoal, provide a tray where the students can deposit these materials for drying.

DESIGNING A FILTRATION SYSTEM

You and your team are going to be designing a two-stage water filtration system as requested in the letter from our client. The first stage will be a synthetic system designed to remove the large objects from the water before it is directed into the second stage. The second stage will be a biological filter, an ecosystem in a field, that removes microscopic contamination from the water before releasing it into the river.

To accomplish this task within the given time frame, you are going to have to split into two subgroups. One group will be working on stage 1 while the other group is working on stage 2. At the end you will come back together as a group to create a short presentation about how the two elements work together.

First, decide how the group is going to break into subgroups. Then decide which subgroup is going to undertake each task. Once you have made these decisions, ask your teacher for the Student Instruction pages for stages 1 and 2.

BUILDING THE STAGE 1 WATER FILTER
STUDENT INSTRUCTIONS

You and your team are to design a multi-barrier system that is completely enclosed. You will need to work as efficiently as possible, both in terms of materials and time. Those groups who get through task 3 quickly will be able to adjust their design before the final test.

TASKS

1. Research the materials
2. Draw your design

3. Build
4. Test
5. Redesign
6. Rebuild
7. Test

MATERIALS

Amounts that you can use are in parentheses. The items in bold type are not included in the material limit.

Coffee filter (1–3)
Pea gravel (¼–¾ cup)
Sand (¼–¾ cup)
Aquarium charcoal (1–3 tablespoons)
Cotton balls (5–20)
Gauze pads (1–3)
Paper towels (1–3)
Scotch tape
Masking tape

TASK 1: RESEARCH

Divide up the list of materials between the group members. Each person needs to research their material to determine how it could be useful in a filter. This may not require you to actually research an item. You may just have to spend time thinking about how it could be useful (e.g., paper towels).

MATERIAL	USEFULNESS IN A FILTER
Coffee filter	_____
Pea gravel	_____
Sand	_____
Aquarium charcoal	_____
Cotton balls	_____
Gauze	_____
Paper towels	_____

TASK 2: DRAW

You need to create a drawing of your filter before you begin building. You are going to build your filter in a funnel for the test, so you need to limit the diameter of your design to 7 centimeters. You also need to include a hypothetical drain (you will not be building this part) in the bottom of the tank (beaker) that would allow water to drain from the stage 1 filter into the stage 2 filter. At the time of testing your filter will need to be enclosed on all sides so the materials stay together while the water flows through the device. However, for your drawing you need to separate the filter into layers and label what materials will be present in what order. You are limited to the use of four of the listed materials above. It is important that you choose carefully because you will need to be able to justify your choice of materials in the space below. Be sure you draw neatly, label all the parts of your filter, and indicate how much of each material you intend to use. Your teacher has final approval of your design and may require you to reduce your material usage if you are being wasteful.

MATERIAL	QUANTITY	REASON FOR THIS MATERIAL
_____	_____	_____
_____	_____	_____
_____	_____	_____
_____	_____	_____

Draw your design in the space below.

TASK 3: BUILD

Now that you have a design, you are ready to build. Everyone in your subgroup must work together to build the filter. Work quickly, but carefully. You need to build your filter from your design, using the materials you chose and placing them in the order indicated on the drawing. Your filter is going to be built in the funnel, so make sure there is room for the water to be poured on top of the filter materials. Be sure to clean up after yourselves; you can't leave a mess for someone else to deal with later!

TASK 4: TESTING

Now that you have successfully created a water filtration device, it is time to see how well it works. Let your teacher know you are ready to test, and get a beaker. Once you have placed the funnel into the beaker, get the safety equipment your teacher requires, then get the 150 mL of testing liquid from your teacher. Before testing, be sure to make observations of the liquid and record what you observe about the color and smell.

REMEMBER! This is a lab activity and lab materials are not to be consumed. Do not drink this water!

Just before you test your filter, decide which of you will do the pouring and which will do the timing. It is very important that the person who does the timing starts the stopwatch as soon as water is being poured and stops when the drip of water out of the bottom has slowed to one drip every 30 seconds. After you have stopped the timer, let your teacher know your test is finished so they can do the necessary grading.

Time it took for water to move through the filter: _____

After your teacher has completed the grading, approach your apparatus and start making some observations in the space below. What does your filter look like after testing? Take the filter out of the funnel and take it apart. What do you notice about the individual components? Did they change in shape, color, or texture due to the test?

Observations:

Dispose of the filter components as instructed by your teacher. Now take a look at the liquid in the bottom of the beaker. Use correct lab measurement techniques to determine how much of the 150 mL of water traveled through the filter. Make observations on the appearance and smell of the liquid. (Remember: Do not drink this water!) Once you have finished making your observations, dispose of the liquid as instructed by your teacher.

Amount of water in the bottom of the beaker: _____

Math break: Now that you have the volume of water that made it through the filter and how long it took, you can figure out the answers to some interesting questions.

1. What is the flow rate for your filter? (Hint: Divide the volume by time.)

2. Given that flow rate, how much water could pass through your filter in 1 hour?

3. How much water could pass through your filter in 1 day (24 hours)?

Now let's pretend that your model is 100 times smaller than the real water filter.

4. How much water could pass through the real filter in 1 hour?

5. How much water could pass through the real filter in 1 day (24 hours)?

TASK 5: REDESIGN

If your group completes the test and there is class time remaining, you will redesign your filter. You don't have to start completely from scratch. Think about what worked well and keep those components. However, if there were things that didn't work as planned, then change those parts. Every filter can be improved, so even if you think your filter was perfect, find a way to make it better. You will need to create a new drawing to go with your new filter. Do not erase your first drawing or add to it. You have to make a second drawing. Make sure you look back at task 1 and include all of the required components.

MATERIAL	QUANTITY	REASON FOR THIS MATERIAL
_____	_____	_____
_____	_____	_____
_____	_____	_____
_____	_____	_____

Draw your design in the space below.

TASK 6: REBUILD

Follow the instructions for task 3.

TASK 7: RETEST

Follow the instructions for task 4.

Time it took for water to move through the filter: _____

Observations:

Amount of water in the bottom of the beaker: _____

Math break: Now that you have the volume of water that made it through the filter and how long it took, you can figure out the answers to some interesting questions.

1. What is the flow rate for your filter? (Hint: Divide the volume by time.)

2. Given that flow rate, how much water could pass through your filter in 1 hour?

3. How much water could pass through your filter in 1 day (24 hours)?

Now let's pretend that your model is 100 times smaller than the real water filter.

4. How much water could pass through the real filter in 1 hour?

5. How much water could pass through the real filter in 1 day (24 hours)?

COMPARISON

Now that you have finished your water filter, let's see how it compares to some commercially available filters. Do you have a Brita filter at home? Brita filters are used by a lot of people to filter their water. Use a search engine to find out what a Brita filter is made of. How does this compare to the materials that are in your filter?

DECONSTRUCTION OF THE RUBRIC

Below you will find how your score in the rubric will be determined. These are the items that will be graded. Make sure they are incorporated in your project.

DRAWING

1. Quality of drawing: The drawing is done neatly. No visible erasure marks. If a line is supposed to be straight, you used a ruler. All elements are large enough that they can be easily seen. The lengths of edges are labeled.

2. Use of materials: The chosen materials are labeled in the drawing, quantities of materials are listed, and there is an explanation for each material chosen.

BUILDING

1. Quality of group work: Everyone in the group is an active participant. The work area is cleaned up after each class period.

2. Appearance of filter: Filter is the correct circumference, looks like the drawing, and is completely enclosed.

TESTING

1. Quality of observations: Volume of filter water is measured. Description of water before and after is included.

2. How well the filter operates: Attached to the side of the beaker. Stays together in one piece.

3. Quality of group work: Everyone in the group is an active participant. The work area is cleaned up after each class period.

TABLE 4.4. *Designing a Two-Stage Water Filter Unit, Grading Rubric for Stage 1*

	EXCELLENT (13-16)	**GOOD (9-12)**	**ACCEPTABLE (5-8)**	**POOR (0-4)**
Drawing	The drawing has a professional quality, and the material usage was well thought out.	The drawing is very well done. The material usage was carefully considered.	The drawing is missing some elements. There didn't seem to be any consideration when choosing materials.	The drawing is missing many elements. There was no thought put into the choosing of materials.
Building	The group worked very well together and cleaned up after themselves. The filter is the right size and looks exactly like the drawing.	The group work well together and cleaned up after themselves. The filter is the right size and looks almost like the drawing.	The group didn't work together very well and did not always clean up after themselves.	The group didn't work together and did not clean up after themselves.
Testing	The group made excellent observations. The water is lighter in color after going through the filter than it was at the beginning of the test.	The group made good observations. The water is lighter in color after going through the filter than it was at the beginning of the test.	The group made less than adequate observations. The water is not lighter in color after going through the filter than it was at the beginning of the test.	The group made inadequate observations. The water is not lighter in color after going through the filter than it was at the beginning of the test

DESIGNING THE STAGE 2 BIOLOGICAL FILTER
STUDENT INSTRUCTIONS

You are going to design a small ecosystem that will serve as the second stage in your filtration system. **Important!** This portion of the filter does not go into the pipe. It is a field that your stage 1 filter will release water into.

While this portion of the filter project is purely design and does not require building, it still requires your attention to detail. There are several components you will have to research in order to identify the most compatible options.

The first thing you will need to include in your plan is a type of soil that will maximize the filtration while minimizing the amount of time for drainage. Then, you will need to include all of the components of an ecosystem. The plants and animals you choose to include will need food sources and predators in order to keep the ecosystem healthy.

TASK 1: RESEARCH

You need to use your best research skills to determine what kind of soil would be best to serve as a filtration device. Be sure to include at least two reasons for your choice.

Next, determine three types of plants what would be found in your ecosystem. Remember that plants have requirements when it comes to temperature, sun, and amount of available water. Make sure your plants could survive in the local area. Be sure to explain why plants are a necessary component in your filtration system.

Decomposers have a vital role in the ecosystem. Research carefully and choose two that would fit our needs as well as be able to survive in the local climate. There must be controls on growth in any ecosystem. Therefore, identify two types of herbivores that could survive in the climate and feed on the plants you have chosen.

Next, determine two carnivores or omnivores that could survive in the climate and could feed on other members of the ecosystem. Be sure each member of the ecosystem has at least one source of food and all but one have a predator. For each organism, write a short description of why you included it in your ecosystem.

You will be expected to cite your sources as determined by your teacher.

Put your research in the space below.

Make sure you read the directions above carefully so that you are researching the right animals.

TASK 2: FOOD WEB DIAGRAM

You are going to take the nine organisms from your ecosystem and create a food web. You may draw pictures of the organisms, or you may simply name the organism. Make sure you fill out the sheet of paper with your food web and make the pictures (label with name of organism) and writing neat and large enough to be seen from a distance.

Paste a picture of your food web in the space below.

TASK 3: DRAWING

Task 3 involves the original filtration system plan you and your entire group made on the first day. That was a rough draft. You need to use that draft as a guide for making the final draft. Make sure the drawing fills the paper and is neatly illustrated. You should include the first stage filter, the drainage pipe that will transport water from the first stage to the second, the second stage filter (which should include the names of the organisms in the approximate place they will be found), and the river.

Paste a picture of your drawing in the space below.

DECONSTRUCTION OF THE RUBRIC

Below you will find how your score in the rubric will be determined. These are the items that will be graded. Make sure they are incorporated in your project.

TABLE 4.5. *Designing a Two-Stage Water Filter Unit, Grading Criteria for Stage 2*

	EXCELLENTS (14–18)	**GOOD (9–13)**	**ACCEPTABLE (5–8)**	**POOR (0–4)**
Research	The research is of excellent quality. All sources have been correctly cited.	The research is of good quality. Most sources have been correctly cited.	The research is of acceptable quality. Some of the sources have been correctly cited.	The research is of poor quality. Few of the sources have been correctly cited.
Food web	All relationships are correctly identified within the food web. All members of the food web are neatly identified.	Most of the relationships are correctly identified within the food web. Most of the members of the food web are neatly identified.	Some of the relationships are correctly identified within the food web. Some of the members of the food web are neatly identified.	Few of the relationships are correctly identified within the food web. Few of the members of the food web are neatly identified.
Drawing of the filtration layout	The drawing has a professional quality and all required elements are present.	The drawing is well done and many of the required elements are present.	The drawing is acceptable and several of the required elements are present.	The drawing is poorly done and most of the required elements are missing.

RESEARCH

1. Quality of work: All required information has been located and neatly written.

2. Sources: You have the proper citation for each source you used.

FOOD WEB

1. Representation of relationships: There are visible arrows present between members of the food web. The arrows point from the thing that is being used for energy toward the organism that is using it for energy.

2. Members of the web: All required members are present. They are represented either by a very neatly drawn picture or by a neatly written name.

DRAWING

1. The drawing is done neatly: No visible erasure marks. If a line is supposed to be straight, you used a ruler. All elements are large enough that they can be easily seen.

2. Required content: The drawing contains the first stage filter, the connection between first stage and second stage, the second stage filter, and the connection between the second stage filter and the river.

TABLE 4.6. *Designing a Two-Stage Water Filter Unit, Grading Criteria for Presentation*

	EXCELLENT (7–8)	**GOOD (5–6)**	**ACCEPTABLE (3–4)**	**POOR (1–2)**
Materials	All materials were included in the presentation. The group was able to integrate the two filter stages into a cohesive whole. The explanations and descriptions were well done and understandable.	All materials were included in the presentation. The group was able to integrate the two filter stages into a cohesive whole. Most of the explanations and descriptions were well done and understandable.	Most of the materials were included in the presentation. The group was not able to integrate the two filter stages into a cohesive whole. Some of the explanations and descriptions were understandable.	Some of the materials were included in the presentation. The group was not able to integrate the two filter stages into a cohesive whole. Few of the explanations and descriptions were understandable.
Behavior	All group members were an active part of the presentation. All group members were well-behaved during the presentation.	Most group members were an active part of the presentation. All group members were well-behaved during the presentation.	Most group members were an active part of the presentation. Most group members were well-behaved during the presentation.	Few group members were an active part of the presentation. Few group members were well-behaved during the presentation.

PRESENTATION GUIDELINES FOR STUDENTS

Your group is going to present all your hard work to the class. You need to include all of the following information in your presentation:

- The picture of your stage 1 filter
- An explanation of how you made your stage 1 filter
- An explanation of why you chose the materials in your stage 1 filter
- A description of how well your stage 1 filter worked
- An idea of how you could make your stage 1 filter work better
- The picture of your stage 2 filter
- An explanation of the components of your stage 2 filter
- A description of why you made your stage 2 filter the way you did
- The picture of your entire filtration system
- An explanation of how the two stages of filters work together to make a whole filtration network

Designing Sunscreen

BY VALARIE BOGAN, SHELBI SMEATHERS, AND S. SELCEN GUZEY

UNIT OVERVIEW

GRADE LEVEL: 7th grade

APPROXIMATE TIME NEEDED TO COMPLETE UNIT:
14 class periods (700 minutes)

UNIT SUMMARY:
Through learning about the cell cycle and the mutations that can occur during the cell cycle, students will understand how these errors can lead to cancer.

STANDARDS ADDRESSED

INDIANA STATE STANDARDS IN LIFE SCIENCE

7.LS2 Develop and use a model to describe the function of a cell as a whole and ways parts of cells contribute to the function.

NEXT GENERATION SCIENCE STANDARDS

MS-LS1-1 Conduct an investigation to provide evidence that living things are made of cells; either one cell or many different numbers and types of cells.

MS-LS1-5 Construct a scientific explanation based on evidence for how environmental and genetic factors influence the growth of organisms.

MS-ETS1-1 Define the criteria and constraints of a design problem with sufficient precision to ensure a successful solution, taking into account relevant scientific principles and potential impacts on people and the natural environment that may limit possible solutions.

MS-ETS1-2 Evaluate competing design solutions using a systematic process to determine how well they meet the criteria and constraints of the problem.

MS-ETS1-3 Analyze data from tests to determine similarities and differences among several design solutions to identify the best characteristics of each that can be combined into a new solution to better meet the criteria for success.

MS-ETS1-4 Develop a model to generate data for iterative testing and modification of a proposed object, tool, or process such that an optimal design can be achieved.

LESSONS

 Lesson 1: Introduction to the Challenge
 Lesson 2: Cell Division
 Lesson 3: What Causes Cancer?
 Lesson 4: Creation of Sunscreen
 Lesson 5: Shark Tank

SAMPLE LESSON PLANS (LESSONS 1, 4, AND 5)

TABLE 4.7. *Designing Sunscreen Unit, Lesson 1*

LESSON 1	INTRODUCTION TO THE CHALLENGE
TIME REQUIRED	**LESSON SUMMARY**
50 min.	This lesson is an introduction to the engineering design process, the engineering challenge, and overall problem framing. Students will frame the problem and use the client letter to set up the next steps of the unit.
STANDARDS ADDRESSED	
Indiana State Standards in Life Science	
7.LS1-2 Develop and use a model to describe the function of a cell as a whole and ways parts of cells contribute to the function.	
Next Generation Science Standards	
MS-ETS1-1 Define the criteria and constraints of a design problem with sufficient precision to ensure a successful solution, taking into account relevant scientific principles and potential impacts on people and the natural environment that may limit possible solutions.	
VOCABULARY	**OBJECTIVE**
Constraint Criteria Engineer Engineering Engineering design process	Students will be able to identify the engineering problem and break it down into the important components.
SAFETY CONSIDERATIONS	
N/A	
BEFORE THE LESSON	
1. Provide access to What a Chemical Engineer Does (see below). 2. Provide access to the design process page (see figure 4.1). 3. Provide access to the client letter (see below). 4. Copy the Problem Scoping Worksheet (see below).	
ASSESSMENTS	**CLASSROOM INSTRUCTIONS**
PRE-ACTIVITY ASSESSMENT	**INTRODUCTION**
N/A	Have students read through the paragraph on chemical engineers. Also give them access to the phone design process image (figure 4.1) so they can read through the descriptors.

ACTIVITY EMBEDDED ASSESSMENT	ACTIVITIES
Listen to student responses throughout individual and class discussion.	*Review Design Process* **Ask:** You read a paragraph about chemical engineers. Who can summarize what this type of engineer does for the class? *Allow students to respond and share.* **Discuss:** Review design phone image (figure 4.1) with students. Use engineering design process provided (figure 4.1). **Say:** You are going to be working on an engineering design problem that concerns skin cancer. **Ask:** How is skin cancer related to mitosis? *Answer:* Too much exposure to UV waves leads to mistakes in mitosis, which leads to the formation of cancer cells. **Ask:** What is the difference in severity between melanoma and nonmelanoma skin cancers? *Answer:* Nonmelanoma doesn't spread and is easily removed, while melanoma spreads easily and is difficult to treat. *Share Letter from Client (Information Gathering)* **Say:** I have a letter for you from our client. It contains a lot of very important information about our project. Please read it silently. *Allow 5 minutes for students to read the letter.* **Say:** Now you are going to act as engineers to frame the problem in small groups (no larger than four). *Allow students time to work to frame the problem using the Problem Scoping Worksheet (see below).* Come back together as a whole group to discuss and collect responses, to come to consensus as a class (information gathering). *Lead Discussion as a Class* It is critical that students are encouraged to share many perspectives on the problem. You should encourage them to think differently about each question. **Ask:** Who did you identify as the client? *Answer:* Dr. Pamela Lie or Derma Worldwide. **Ask:** What is the problem? *Answer:* Need to develop once-a-day natural sunscreen. **Ask:** What is the client asking for? *Answer:* A sunscreen formula. Evidence for why they should choose your formula. **Ask:** Who will benefit from your product? *Answer:* Anyone who uses sunscreen. **Ask:** What are the requirements (criteria) and limitations (constraints)? *Answer:* Use the engineering design process. Product must be reliable. Process must demonstrate the use of scientific reasoning.
POST-ACTIVITY ASSESSMENT	**CLOSURE**
N/A	Review steps of design process achieved so far and prep for moving on to digging deeper in subsequent classes. **Ask:** So far, where are we in the design process? *Allow students to respond. Students should identify the EXPLOREit phase.*

	Say: Tomorrow, we will dig deeper and take a look at some of the content pieces the client asked that we discuss. **Ask:** What did the client say we will need to be learning? *Refer students to section of client letter where client discusses what teacher needs to teach students.*
ASSESSMENTS CONTINUED	
N/A	
EDUCATOR RESOURCES	
N/A	

WHAT A CHEMICAL ENGINEER DOES

"Chemical engineering is all about turning raw materials into useful, everyday products. The clothes we wear, the food and drink we consume and the energy we use all depend upon chemical engineering. Chemical engineers work out the processes to make all these products, while also helping to manage the world's resources, protect the environment and ensure health and safety standards are met. Most jobs in the sector fall into one of two groups: the design, manufacture, and operation of plants and machinery, or the development of new or adapted substances and materials."

Excerpt from Samantha Tyson, "So, What Does a Chemical Engineer Do, Exactly?," *Guardian Professional*, February 12, 2013, https://www.theguardian.com/careers/what-chemical-engineer-does.

CLIENT LETTER

Dear Student Engineers:

Skin cancer is the most common type of cancer in the United States. In fact, the majority of cases are caused by exposure to ultraviolet (UV) radiation from the sun and therefore are largely preventable. Getting exposed to UV radiation from tanning beds has also increased the risk of skin cancer. So, tanning beds are not safe.

There are two types of skin cancer: melanoma and nonmelanoma. A study by Mayo Clinic shows that between the years 2000 and 2010, there was an approximate 200 percent increase in the number of nonmelanoma cases. There has also been a significant increase in melanoma cases, 800 percent among young women and 400 percent among young men. Melanoma cancers are more dangerous than nonmelanoma cancers because melanoma is much more likely to spread to other parts of the body.

Laboratory research has helped us understand how UV radiation affects skin cells. UV rays damage the skin cells' DNA, potentially causing mutations that may lead to cancer. Regular daily use of an SPF 30 or higher sunscreen reduces the risk of developing melanoma by 75 percent.

While you can find many different types of sunscreen products on the market, some of them are full of harmful chemicals and some are not as effective as others. Over the last few years, in partnership with scientists at Purdue University, engineers at our skin care research and development company have developed and tested new, once-a-day, natural sunscreen products to meet the demands of many consumers. We are at capacity in our ability to keep up with all of the work in the area of sun protection products. I want to enlist your help to provide us with a safe and effective sunscreen formula.

Please use the engineering design process, science knowledge, and your ingenuity to develop a product for us. Please also provide us with evidence for why your design is the one we should move forward with. Please note that your development of your sunscreen product must be timely and reliable, and it must demonstrate the use of scientific reasoning. We are looking forward to seeing what you develop.

Sincerely,
Pamela M. Lie, MD, PhD
Chief Executive Officer
Derma Worldwide

PROBLEM SCOPING WORKSHEET
WHAT? HOW? WHY?

DIRECTIONS: With your group, construct a response to each of the following questions using information from the client letter.

1. Who is the client?

2. What is the client's problem that needs a solution? Be certain to explain why this problem is important to solve. Use information from the client to support your reasons.

3. Who will benefit from your product (end users)?

4. What are the requirements for the sunscreen? Use detailed information from the client.

5. What did the client say you need to learn, and your teacher needs to teach you about, in order to solve this problem?

TABLE 4.8. *Designing Sunscreen Unit, Lesson 4, Part I*

LESSON 4, DAY 1	CREATION OF SUNSCREEN
TIME REQUIRED	LESSON SUMMARY
50 min.	Students will conduct research to develop and test three sunscreen formulations. The research will help students to create a presentation that details the steps of mitosis and specifies how mutations in cells can cause cancer.
STANDARDS ADDRESSED	
Indiana State Standards in Life Science 7.LS1-2 Develop and use a model to describe the function of a cell as a whole and ways parts of cells contribute to the function. **Next Generation Science Standards** MS-LS1-5 Construct a scientific explanation based on evidence for how environmental and genetic factors influence the growth of organisms. MS-ETS1-2 Evaluate competing design solutions using a systematic process to determine how well they meet the criteria and constraints of the problem.	

MS-ETS1-3 Analyze data from tests to determine similarities and differences among several design solutions to identify the best characteristics of each that can be combined into a new solution to better meet the criteria for success.

MS-ETS1-4 Develop a model to generate data for iterative testing and modification of a proposed object, tool, or process such that an optimal design can be achieved.

VOCABULARY	OBJECTIVE
Castor oil Shea butter UV beads Zinc oxide	Students will conduct research for materials for their sunscreen formula.

BEFORE THE LESSON
Documents needed for today: Background Research Worksheet (see below).

ASSESSMENTS	CLASSROOM INSTRUCTIONS
PRE-ACTIVITY ASSESSMENT	**INTRODUCTION**
Hold a class discussion. See question suggestions in the box to the right.	Review the client letter and other materials. **Ask:** Who is our client? *Answer:* Derma Worldwide. **Ask:** What do they want us to do for them? *Answer:* Design a natural sunscreen. **Ask:** Why do they want us to do this? *Answer:* Number of skin cancer cases is increasing. A need for more natural sunscreens. **Ask:** What have we learned about the cell cycle that could be important to the creation of our sunscreen? *Answer:* Cells spend most of their time not dividing and are vulnerable to the effect of the sun's rays. So, we need to protect the cells from harmful rays. **Ask:** What have we learned about cancer and the cell cycle that is important to the development of our sunscreen? *Answer:* Cancer causes mutations, which cause cells to continually divide. So, cells need to be protected from UV radiation, which can cause mutations. *Share the agenda for the day with the students.* **Ask:** Where are we in the design process? *Answer:* LEARNIt.
ACTIVITY EMBEDDED ASSESSMENT	**ACTIVITIES**
While the students are working, walk around and ask the following questions: • What qualities does that material have that will make it a good choice for your sunscreen? *Answer:* Make sure they explain why these qualities make it a good choice.	After you have assigned groups, have them divide up the materials and begin the research process. Make sure that each group records their information on the Background Research Worksheet. As you walk around the room, carry one of the materials with you, allowing the students to smell it as you pass by. Continue substituting materials until they have had the opportunity to smell each one. **It is very important** that the students use the provided information resource page for their research. A great deal of time was spent compiling the best resources for this task.

• How is that material going to protect cells from UV radiation? *Answer:* It is either a physical or chemical barrier.	
POST-ACTIVITY ASSESSMENT	**CLOSURE**
See details in the box to the right.	Exit ticket: What did you learn? What do you still need to learn?

BACKGROUND RESEARCH WORKSHEET

Today you are going to start the process of developing a sunscreen that can protect cells from the damaging rays of the sun while also having a pleasing texture and smell.

MATERIALS RESEARCH

You have probably never worked with these materials before today. When an engineer encounters unusual materials, they research these items individually to determine the characteristics that will affect their future projects.

Today you are going to do the same thing. You and your group mates are going to divide up the potential materials and research each of them to determine the following: whether the material protects the cells from the rays of the sun; if possible, how the material protects the cells from the rays of the sun; how the material is typically used in skin care; and which materials would be used for fragrance.

MATERIALS TO RESEARCH

Coconut oil
Castor oil
Shea butter
Beeswax
Almond oil
Sesame seed oil
Peppermint oil
Aloe
Zinc oxide
Olive oil

MATERIAL	WHO RESEARCHED	HOW IT PROTECTS AGAINST THE SUN	WHY IT IS GOOD FOR SKIN CARE	FRAGRANCE
Coconut oil				
Castor oil				
Shea butter				
Beeswax				
Almond oil				
Sesame seed oil				
Peppermint oil				
Aloe				
Zinc oxide				
Olive oil				

TABLE 4.9. Designing Sunscreen Unit, Lesson 4, Part 2	
LESSON 4, DAY 2	**CREATION OF SUNSCREEN**
TIME REQUIRED	**LESSON SUMMARY**
50 min.	Students will be working individually as well as in groups to determine the best formula for their sunscreen. They will be creating that formula by the end of the class period.
STANDARDS ADDRESSED	
Indiana State Standards in Life Science	
7.LS1-2 Develop and use a model to describe the function of a cell as a whole and ways parts of cells contribute to the function.	
Next Generation Science Standards	
MS-LS1-5 Construct a scientific explanation based on evidence for how environmental and genetic factors influence the growth of organisms. **MS-ETS1-2** Evaluate competing design solutions using a systematic process to determine how well they meet the criteria and constraints of the problem. **MS-ETS1-3** Analyze data from tests to determine similarities and differences among several design solutions to identify the best characteristics of each that can be combined into a new solution to better meet the criteria for success. **MS-ETS1-4** Develop a model to generate data for iterative testing and modification of a proposed object, tool, or process such that an optimal design can be achieved.	
VOCABULARY	**OBJECTIVES**
Castor oil Shea butter UV beads Zinc oxide	• Students will be able to create an effective formula for sunscreen that prevents UVA and UVB rays from harming cells. • Students will create a presentation that explains how changes to cells by UV rays can lead to cancer.
MATERIALS	
3 hotplates 3 400 mL beakers 3 150 mL beakers	

5 10 mL syringes
7 beakers of any size
5 eyedroppers
Measuring spoons
Graduated cylinder
Dixie cups
Craft sticks
UV beads
UV light bulb
Coconut oil
Castor oil
Shea butter
Beeswax
Almond oil
Sesame seed oil
Peppermint oil
Aloe
Non-nano zinc oxide
Olive oil

SAFETY CONSIDERATIONS

1. The powdered zinc oxide can be a breathing hazard. Therefore, it is imperative that you mix it with olive oil before putting it out for the students to use. Use care as you mix ½ teaspoon of zinc oxide powder with 50 mL of olive oil.
2. To avoid burning dangers, keep the hot plates and water baths in a secure location and only allow students near them under supervision.

BEFORE THE LESSON

Mix the zinc oxide with olive oil, put all ingredients in beakers, set up water baths, and create an assembly line of materials. Also, designate an area where you want the students to place their sunscreens for the night.

Documents needed for today: Teacher Notes for Sunscreen Creation (see below); Student Sunscreen Design Worksheet (see below).

ASSESSMENTS	CLASSROOM INSTRUCTIONS
PRE-ACTIVITY ASSESSMENT	**INTRODUCTION**
Hold a class discussion. See question suggestion in the box to the right.	Share the agenda for the day with the students. **Ask:** Where are we in the design process? *Students should identify the PICKIt and BUILDIt phases.*
ACTIVITY EMBEDDED ASSESSMENT	**ACTIVITIES**
While the groups are designing their sunscreens, walk around and ask the following questions: • Which materials did you choose? • Why do you think those materials are beneficial for your sunscreen?	Each student should begin today by identifying the materials they think are best suited for a sunscreen and giving reasons for those decisions on the individual sunscreen ideas page. (See Sunscreen Design Worksheet below.) Once all students in the group have made some individual decisions, have them come together as a group to design their first sunscreen. Stress that they need to work together to create this formula. One person should not make all the decisions.

• How are these materials going to protect cells from UV radiation?	Once they have created their plan, they need to bring it to you for approval. Be sure to examine the amounts of add-ins they are using to make sure they aren't above the maximum for that product. In addition, if they are using more than the minimum for a product, they need to provide a reason for that choice. If you feel that their reasoning is not valid, have them make changes to their plan. It is important that only two people from the group come to the assembly line. One person will be in charge of calling out the ingredients and amounts to the person collecting the materials. The person calling out should stand back a step or two from the assembly line. The students should place their cups, which have been labeled, in the appropriate place after completing their formula for the day. If a group gets done early, they should start working on the mitosis extravaganza portion of their project. (See Mitosis Extravaganza Worksheet below.)
POST-ACTIVITY ASSESSMENT	**CLOSURE**
See details in the box to the right.	**Ask:** How is your sunscreen going to protect cells from UV radiation? **Ask:** Why is it important to protect cells against UV rays?

TEACHER NOTES FOR SUNSCREEN CREATION

MATERIALS NEEDED IN ADDITION TO THE INGREDIENTS

3 hotplates
3 400 mL beakers
3 150 mL beakers
5 10 mL syringes
7 beakers of any size (use 50–100 mL beakers if you have them, but if you don't any size will do)
5 eyedroppers
Dixie cups
Craft sticks

BASE MATERIALS

The shea butter and coconut oil will have to be melted in a water bath. To do this you will need to fill two of the 400 mL beakers approximately halfway with water and place them onto hot plates. Scoop out enough of the shea butter or coconut oil so that the 150 mL beaker is half filled. Place the smaller beaker inside the larger beaker and turn up the heat. It will not take long for these materials to melt.

Important: Make sure the hot plates are not in an area that is easily accessible to the students.

The students are going to measure out their base material with a syringe. This is an unusual tool, but it should make the process of getting the base material easier than other measurement devices. Make sure the students use the syringe designated for the base material. Cross contamination will cause serious problems with their sunscreen formulation.

ADD-INS

The beeswax will also have to be melted in a water bath (see instructions above). Be aware that the beeswax melts more slowly than the other materials in a water bath.

The zinc oxide can be a breathing hazard for the students if left in its powdered form. In order to alleviate this danger you need to mix 50 mL of olive oil with ½ teaspoon zinc oxide powder. Have students give it a gentle stir before putting the material into the eyedropper. This should be enough to last you for an entire day and possibly longer depending on how often it is chosen by the students.

CREATING THE MATERIALS ASSEMBLY LINE

You will need a lab bench or long table for the assembly line. Put all four base materials next to each other but with enough space for a student to stand in front of each material. The materials on a hot plate should be carefully monitored by an adult. The materials on a hot plate need a syringe while the materials in other beakers need eyedroppers.

The add-ins should be separated from the base materials. There is one material that requires a hot plate. It should be placed closest to the base materials and closely monitored. This material will have an eyedropper with it, not a syringe. Place the rest of the add-ins in a line, again leaving enough space that a student could stand in front of each material.

PROCEDURES FOR ASSEMBLY LINE

Before a group makes their sunscreen, you need to check their plan. If they are using more than the minimum of the add-in materials, you need to check their reasoning. One person from a group should make the sunscreen in a Dixie cup. The other group members should remain in their work area to reduce the danger of things being knocked over or broken.

SUNSCREEN DESIGN WORKSHEET

A. SUNSCREEN MATERIAL CHOICES

Now that you have researched and discussed the merits of individual materials, it is time to create a sunscreen. The base material will make up the majority of your sunscreen. It should have the qualities you want in your sunscreen. The add-ins will act to increase the UV protection of your sunscreen but must be used in small amounts. You will get 3 mL of the base material, but you may select the amount of the add-in to use. The range of amounts are listed in parentheses after the add-in. Bear in mind that you will have to provide justification for using more than the minimum amount.

BASE MATERIAL CHOICES (CHOOSE ONLY 1)

- Olive oil
- Castor oil
- Shea butter
- Coconut oil

ADD-INS (YOU MAY CHOOSE 3)

- Aloe (1–5 drops)

Almond oil (1–5 drops)
Beeswax (10–30 drops)
Peppermint oil (1–5 drops)
Sesame seed oil (1–5 drops)
Zinc oxide (1–5 drops)

B. INDIVIDUAL SUNSCREEN IDEAS

Before you start working with your group, you need to decide which ingredients you think are most effective at making a sunscreen.

MOST IMPORTANT INGREDIENTS

Identify four of the ingredients you think are most important in a sunscreen and identify the reasons for your decision. (Hint: Be sure to use the group research to make your decision.)

INGREDIENT
_____
_____
_____
_____

REASON
_____
_____
_____
_____

CRITERIA

What characteristics are important to you in a sun protection product?

C. SUNSCREEN DESIGN

Now that everyone in your group has had a chance to think about the sunscreen during the individual sunscreen ideas activity, it is time to come to a consensus within your group and develop your first sunscreen formula.

You must be able to justify each of your choices, and if you are using more than the minimum amount you must justify why you need the extra material.

BASE MATERIAL: _____
  Amount: _____
  Reason for choice: _____
  Reason for amount: _____

ADD-IN: _____
  Amount: _____
  Reason for choice: _____
  Reason for amount: _____

ADD-IN: _____
  Amount: _____

Reason for choice: _____

Reason for amount: _____

ADD-IN: _____

Amount: _____

Reason for choice: _____

Reason for amount: _____

PROCEDURES FOR CREATING YOUR SUNSCREEN

1. Get a Dixie cup, a marker, and a craft stick. Write your group name and class period on the cup.
2. Get your teacher's approval for your plan.
3. Assemble your sunscreen quickly. Start by getting 3 mL of your base material in your cup and then put in your additional materials. Be sure to count the drops of your add-ins carefully and go slowly!
4. As soon as all of your materials are in the cup, stir quickly and thoroughly.
5. Place your formulation where instructed to by your teacher. Your sunscreen must sit overnight before it can be tested.

TESTING STEPS

1. Pick up your group's Dixie cup and a UV bead.
2. Thoroughly cover your UV bead with your sunscreen. Put it on a small piece of paper that contains your group name and place it in front of the UV light. You need to leave your bead in front of the lamp for 5 minutes. Go on to step 3 while you wait.
3. Now you need to document the qualities of your sunscreen.

    a. Place a little of your sunscreen between your fingers and rub them together. What does your sunscreen feel like? In other words, what is its texture?

    b. What color is it?

    c. What does it smell like?

    d. How easy is it to spread? (Use the craft stick to spread a little on a piece of paper.)

    e. Is there anything else remarkable about your sunscreen formula?

4. After 5 minutes have passed, observe the color of your bead. Make sure you place the used bead in the cup your teacher designated for that purpose.
5. What was the outcome of your test? In other words, what color did your bead turn?
    Be sure to throw away your Dixie cup and craft stick.

MITOSIS EXTRAVAGANZA WORKSHEET

As part of your Shark Tank presentation, you will need to tell the judges about mitosis and how mutations in cells can lead to cancer.

You and your group are going to plan your mitosis presentation. If you have ever seen the show "Shark Tank," you know that the presenters use a lot of energy to present their product. You'll need to channel some creative energy for this presentation. Think about creating a song, dance, computer animation, skit, or colorful artistic display that presents mitosis.

Your presentation should include the following:
- Interphase (including the G1 and G2 checkpoints)
- Anaphase
- Prophase
- Telophase
- Metaphase
- How mutations affect mitosis and how they can lead to cancer

TABLE 4.10. *Designing Sunscreen Unit, Lesson 4, Part 3*

LESSON 4, DAY 3	CREATION OF SUNSCREEN
TIME REQUIRED	LESSON SUMMARY
50 min.	Students will be testing their sunscreen formula, then taking information gained from that test to redesign the formula. They will also be working on an artistic representation of mitosis.
STANDARDS ADDRESSED	
INDIANA STATE STANDARDS IN LIFE SCIENCE 7.LS1-2 Develop and use a model to describe the function of a cell as a whole and ways parts of cells contribute to the function. **Next Generation Science Standards** MS-LS1-5 Construct a scientific explanation based on evidence for how environmental and genetic factors influence the growth of organisms. MS-ETS1-2 Evaluate competing design solutions using a systematic process to determine how well they meet the criteria and constraints of the problem. MS-ETS1-3 Analyze data from tests to determine similarities and differences among several design solutions to identify the best characteristics of each that can be combined into a new solution to better meet the criteria for success. MS-ETS1-4 Develop a model to generate data for iterative testing and modification of a proposed object, tool, or process such that an optimal design can be achieved.	
VOCABULARY	OBJECTIVES
Castor oil Shea butter UV beads Zinc oxide	• Students will be able to create and test an effective formula for sunscreen that prevents UVA and UVB rays from harming cells. • Students will create a presentation that explains how changes to cells by UV rays can lead to cancer.
MATERIALS	
3 hotplates 3 400 mL beakers 3 150 mL beakers 5 10 mL syringes	

7 beakers of any size 5 eyedroppers Measuring spoons Graduated cylinder Dixie cups Craft sticks UV beads UV light bulb Coconut oil Castor oil Shea butter Beeswax Almond oil Sesame seed oil Peppermint oil Aloe Non-nano zinc oxide Olive oil	

SAFETY CONSIDERATIONS	

1. The powdered zinc oxide can be a breathing hazard. Therefore, it is imperative that you mix it with olive oil before putting it out for the students to use. Use care as you mix ½ teaspoon of zinc oxide powder with 50 mL of olive oil.
2. To avoid burning dangers, keep the hot plates and water baths in a secure location and only allow students near them under supervision.

BEFORE THE LESSON	

Set up the material assembly line as described above. In addition, put out the UV light bulb for testing purposes. You will need to put out a container for the used UV beads. These are going to be reused, so do not have the students throw them away!

Documents needed for today: Sunscreen Redesign Worksheet (see below).

ASSESSMENTS	CLASSROOM INSTRUCTIONS
PRE-ACTIVITY ASSESSMENT	**INTRODUCTION**
Hold a class discussion. See question suggestion in the box to the right.	Share the agenda for the day with the students. **Ask:** Where are we in the design process? *Students should identify the TRYIt phase.*
ACTIVITY EMBEDDED ASSESSMENT	**ACTIVITIES**
Walk around the room and ask groups the following questions: • What were some good qualities of your sunscreen? • What were some things that needed to be improved? • What material do you think could supply that improvement?	Students will need to start the period by getting their sunscreen and testing it in accordance with the instructions on the Sunscreen Design Worksheet. Be sure to have a container for the used UV beads. Do not place the container in a sink or you will have UV beads going down the drain. After students have tested their formula, they should use the Sunscreen Redesign Worksheet to design their next formula. Once again, when they are finished with their design, they should get your approval and then create their sunscreen. Be sure each group has reasons for the choices they make for their formula. Once a group has made their second formula, they should put it in the designated place.

• What is the purpose of your sunscreen? *Answer:* To protect cells from UV rays.	At the end of the day, you will need to wash the UV beads. To do this you need a pan with soapy water. Just run the beads through your hands to remove the sunscreen, then rinse them clean and place them on paper towels to dry overnight.
POST-ACTIVITY ASSESSMENT	**CLOSURE**
See details in the box to the right.	Have a quick round-robin where every group shares what worked well and what went badly in the *TRYIt phase*.

SUNSCREEN REDESIGN WORKSHEET

Now you have had your first test. What were some positive outcomes from your test?

What were some negative outcomes from your test?

What can you change to make your sunscreen better? (You can only change one thing.)

Design your formula below. Remember that you must be able to justify each of your choices, and if you are using more than the minimum amount you must justify why you need the extra material.

BASE MATERIAL: _____

    Amount: _____

    Reason for choice: _____

    Reason for amount: _____

ADD-IN: _____

    Amount: _____

    Reason for choice: _____

    Reason for amount: _____

ADD-IN: _____

    Amount: _____

    Reason for choice: _____

    Reason for amount: _____

ADD-IN: _____

    Amount: _____

    Reason for choice: _____

    Reason for amount: _____

PROCEDURES FOR CREATING YOUR SUNSCREEN

1. Get a Dixie cup, a marker, and a craft stick. Write your group name and class period on the cup.
2. Get your teacher's approval for your plan.

3. Assemble your sunscreen quickly. Start by getting 3 mL of your base material in your cup and then put in your additional materials. Be sure to count the drops of your add-ins carefully and go slowly!

4. As soon as all of your materials are in the cup, stir quickly and thoroughly.

5. Place your formulation where instructed to by your teacher. Your sunscreen must sit overnight before it can be tested.

TESTING STEPS

1. Pick up your group's Dixie cup and a UV bead.

2. Thoroughly cover your UV bead with your sunscreen. Put it on a small piece of paper that contains your group name and place it in front of the UV light. You need to leave your bead in front of the lamp for 5 minutes. Go on to step 3 while you wait.

3. Now you need to document the cosmetic qualities of your sunscreen.

   a. Place a little of your sunscreen between your fingers and rub them together. What does your sunscreen feel like? In other words, what is its texture?

   b. What color is it?

   c. What does it smell like?

   d. How easy is it to spread on the back of your hand? (Just one person needs to spread a tiny amount onto their hand.)

   e. Is there anything else remarkable about your sunscreen formula?

4. After 5 minutes have passed, observe the color of your bead. Make sure you place the used bead in the cup your teacher designated for that purpose.

5. What was the outcome of your test? In other words, what color did your bead turn?

Be sure to throw away your Dixie cup and craft stick.

TABLE 4.11. *Designing Sunscreen Unit, Lesson 4, Part 4*

LESSON 4, DAY 4	CREATION OF SUNSCREEN
TIME REQUIRED	LESSON SUMMARY
50 min.	Students will test the redesigned sunscreen and create a last redesign.
STANDARDS ADDRESSED	
Indiana State Standards in Life Science	
7.LS1-2: Develop and use a model to describe the function of a cell as a whole and ways parts of cells contribute to the function.	
Next Generation Science Standards	
MS-LS1-5 Construct a scientific explanation based on evidence for how environmental and genetic factors influence the growth of organisms. MS-ETS1-2 Evaluate competing design solutions using a systematic process to determine how well they meet the criteria and constraints of the problem.	

MS-ETS1-3 Analyze data from tests to determine similarities and differences among several design solutions to identify the best characteristics of each that can be combined into a new solution to better meet the criteria for success.

MS-ETS1-4 Develop a model to generate data for iterative testing and modification of a proposed object, tool, or process such that an optimal design can be achieved.

VOCABULARY	OBJECTIVE
Castor oil Shea butter UV beads Zinc oxide	Students will test the redesign and create a second design.

MATERIALS
3 hotplates 3 400 mL beakers 3 150 mL beakers 5 10 mL syringes 7 beakers of any size 5 eyedroppers Measuring spoons Graduated cylinder Dixie cups Craft sticks UV beads UV light bulb Coconut oil Castor oil Shea butter Beeswax Almond oil Sesame seed oil Peppermint oil Aloe Non-nano zinc oxide Olive oil

SAFETY CONSIDERATIONS
1. The powdered zinc oxide can be a breathing hazard. Therefore, it is imperative that you mix it with olive oil before putting it out for the students to use. Use care as you mix ½ teaspoon of zinc oxide powder with 50 mL of olive oil. 2. To avoid burning dangers, keep the hot plates and water baths in a secure location and only allow students near them under supervision.

BEFORE THE LESSON
Set up the material assembly line as described for Day 2. 　Documents needed for today: Sunscreen Redesign Worksheet (continued from yesterday); Mitosis Extravaganza (continued from yesterday); Sunscreen Last Design Worksheet.

ASSESSMENTS	CLASSROOM INSTRUCTIONS
PRE-ACTIVITY ASSESSMENT	**INTRODUCTION**
Hold a class discussion. See question suggestion in the box to the right.	Share the agenda for the day with the students. **Ask:** Where are we in the design process? *Students should identify the REFINEIt phase.*
ACTIVITY EMBEDDED ASSESSMENT	**ACTIVITIES**

Walk around and ask groups the following questions:
• How do UV rays cause skin cancer?
• How is a cancer cell different from a normal cell?
	This day will be very much like Day 3 with the exception that the students will be testing the redesign and creating a second redesign.
	    Students will need to start the period by getting their sunscreen and testing it in accordance with the instructions on the Sunscreen Redesign Worksheet. Be sure to have a container for the used UV beads. Do not place the container in a sink or you will have UV beads going down the drain.
	    After students have tested their formula, they should use the Sunscreen Last Design Worksheet to design their next formula. Once again, when they are finished, they should get your approval and then create their sunscreen. Be sure each group has reasons for the choices they make for their formula. Once a group has made their last formula, they should put it in the designated place.
	    At the end of the day, you will need to wash the UV beads. To do this you need a pan with soapy water. Just run the beads through your hands to remove the sunscreen then rinse them clean and place them on paper towels to dry overnight.

POST-ACTIVITY ASSESSMENT	**CLOSURE**
See details in the box to the right.	Exit ticket: How do sunscreens protect skin cells from UV light?

SUNSCREEN LAST DESIGN WORKSHEET

Now you have had your second test. What were some positive outcomes from that test?

What were some negative outcomes from that test?

What can you change to make your sunscreen better? (Remember, you can only change one thing.)

Design your formula below. Remember that you must be able to justify each of your choices, and if you are using more than the minimum amount you must justify why you need the extra material.

BASE MATERIAL: _____

    Amount: _____

    Reason for choice: _____

    Reason for amount: _____

ADD-IN: _____

    Amount: _____

    Reason for choice: _____

    Reason for amount: _____

ADD-IN: _____

    Amount: _____

    Reason for choice: _____

    Reason for amount: _____

ADD-IN: _____

    Amount: _____

    Reason for choice: _____

    Reason for amount: _____

PROCEDURES FOR CREATING YOUR SUNSCREEN

1. Get a Dixie cup, a marker, and a craft stick. Write your group name and class period on the cup.
2. Get your teacher's approval for your plan.
3. Assemble your sunscreen quickly. Start by getting 3 mL of your base material in your cup and then put in your additional materials. Be sure to count the drops of your add-ins carefully and go slowly!
4. As soon as all of your materials are in the cup, stir quickly and thoroughly.
5. Place your formulation where instructed to by your teacher. Your sunscreen must sit overnight before it can be tested.

TESTING STEPS

1. Pick up your group's Dixie cup and a UV bead.
2. Thoroughly cover your UV bead with your sunscreen. Put it on a small piece of paper that contains your group name and place it in front of the UV light. You need to leave your bead in front of the lamp for 5 minutes. Go on to step 3 while you wait.
3. Now you need to document the cosmetic qualities of your sunscreen.

    a. Place a little of your sunscreen between your fingers and rub them together. What does your sunscreen feel like? In other words, what is its texture?

    b. What color is it?

    c. What does it smell like?

    d. How easy is it to spread on the back of your hand? (Just one person needs to spread a tiny amount onto their hand.)

    e. Is there anything else remarkable about your sunscreen formula?

4. After 5 minutes have passed, observe the color of your bead. Make sure you place the used bead in the cup your teacher designated for that purpose.
5. What was the outcome of your test? In other words, what color did your bead turn?

Be sure to throw away your Dixie cup and craft stick.

FINAL DECISION TIME

1. Which of the three formulas was the best overall performer? In other words, which one had the best results on the bead, the best texture, the best spreadability, the nicest color, and the nicest smell? Write down the exact formula on a sheet of paper and give it to your teacher.

TABLE 4.12. *Designing Sunscreen Unit, Lesson 4, Part 5*

LESSON 4, DAY 5	CREATION OF SUNSCREEN
TIME REQUIRED	LESSON SUMMARY
50 min.	Students will test the last redesign.
STANDARDS ADDRESSED	
Indiana State Standards in Life Science 7.LS1-2 Develop and use a model to describe the function of a cell as a whole and ways parts of cells contribute to the function. **Next Generation Science Standards** MS-LS1-5 Construct a scientific explanation based on evidence for how environmental and genetic factors influence the growth of organisms. MS-ETS1-2 Evaluate competing design solutions using a systematic process to determine how well they meet the criteria and constraints of the problem. MS-ETS1-3 Analyze data from tests to determine similarities and differences among several design solutions to identify the best characteristics of each that can be combined into a new solution to better meet the criteria for success. MS-ETS1-4 Develop a model to generate data for iterative testing and modification of a proposed object, tool, or process such that an optimal design can be achieved.	
VOCABULARY	OBJECTIVE
Castor oil Shea butter UV beads Zinc oxide	Students will test the last redesign and complete their mitosis presentation.
MATERIALS	
3 hotplates 3 400 mL beakers 3 150 mL beakers 5 10 mL syringes 7 beakers of any size 5 eyedroppers	

Measuring spoons
Graduated cylinder
Dixie cups
Craft sticks
UV beads
UV light bulb
Coconut oil
Castor oil
Shea butter
Beeswax
Almond oil
Sesame seed oil
Peppermint oil
Aloe
Non-nano zinc oxide
Olive oil

SAFETY CONSIDERATIONS
1. The powdered zinc oxide can be a breathing hazard. Therefore, it is imperative that you mix it with olive oil before putting it out for the students to use. Use care as you mix ½ teaspoon of zinc oxide powder with 50 mL of olive oil. 2. To avoid burning dangers, keep the hot plates and water baths in a secure location and only allow students near them under supervision.

BEFORE THE LESSON
Set up the material assembly line as described for Day 2.   Documents needed for today: Sunscreen Redesign Worksheet (continued from yesterday); Mitosis Extravaganza (continued from yesterday); Sunscreen Last Design Worksheet.

ASSESSMENTS	CLASSROOM INSTRUCTIONS
PRE-ACTIVITY ASSESSMENT	**INTRODUCTION**
Hold a class discussion. See question suggestion in the box to the right.	Share the agenda for the day with the students. **Ask:** Where are we in the design process? *Students should identify the REFINEIt phase.*
ACTIVITY EMBEDDED ASSESSMENT	**ACTIVITIES**

Walk around and ask the groups the following questions:
• Why did you choose this formula to present?
• What makes this formula better than the other two?
• How can cells be affected by the UV rays of the sun?
Answer: Can cause mutations that make the checkpoints fail.
	This day is again very similar to Days 3 and 4 except the students will be testing the last redesign.
	    Students will need to start the period by getting their sunscreen and testing it in accordance with the instructions on the Sunscreen Last Design Worksheet.
	    Students will need to choose which formula they are going to present and turn that in to you.

POST-ACTIVITY ASSESSMENT	**CLOSURE**
See details in the box to the right.	Exit ticket: What is one question you still have about mitosis and sunscreen?

TABLE 4.13. *Designing Sunscreen Unit, Lesson 5*

LESSON 5	SHARK TANK
TIME REQUIRED	**LESSON SUMMARY**
200 min. (4 × 50 min. class period)	Students will spend two class periods planning and practicing presentations for the class Shark Tank–style presentations. On Lesson 4, Day 5, they should have picked their formula to present and been preparing their presentations to the class. The focus should be on presenting scientific information and product details to potential investors. Lesson 5 could take 3–4 days depending on the number of student groups and the speed of their presentations.
STANDARDS ADDRESSED	
Next Generation Science Standards	
MS-ETS1-2 Evaluate competing design solutions using a systematic process to determine how well they meet the criteria and constraints of the problem.	
MS-ETS1-3 Analyze data from tests to determine similarities and differences among several design solutions to identify the best characteristics of each that can be combined into a new solution to better meet the criteria for success.	
MS-ETS1-4 Develop a model to generate data for iterative testing and modification of a proposed object, tool, or process such that an optimal design can be achieved.	
VOCABULARY	**OBJECTIVES**
N/A	• Students will share out their formulas and the results of testing during a Shark Tank–style presentation. • Students will evaluate each other's designs using a feedback protocol during presentations
SAFETY CONSIDERATIONS	
N/A	
BEFORE THE LESSON	
1. Print out Determining Cost Worksheet (see below). 2. Print out Presentation Guidelines Worksheet (see below). 3. Print out Presentation Rubric page (see table 4.14 below). 4. Print out Presentation Evaluation page (see below).	
ASSESSMENTS	**CLASSROOM INSTRUCTIONS**
PRE-ACTIVITY ASSESSMENT	**INTRODUCTION**
Ask students where we are in the design process. Listen to responses during discussion.	*Return to Project Groups* **Ask:** Where are we in the design process? *Students should identify that they are near the SHAREIt phase.* *Transition* Today students are going to be returning to the sunscreen formula to create their final presentations. **Say:** Today we are going to begin the final stages of our project. In order to do this, we need to discuss the important aspects of public speaking and presentations.

At this time it would be appropriate to discuss as a class good public speaking techniques and things they think they should include in their presentations. Some questions to ask the group might include:

1. How many of you have spoken in front of a whole class or a group of adults before? What was that experience like? What are some things you did to prepare?
2. How many of you have watched a classmate or an adult give a presentation? What are some things they did well? What would you recommend not to do?
3. What are some things that good presentations have to get and keep your attention?
4. What are the worst types of presentations? Why are they so bad?
5. What are some things that you know about presenting a product for sale? *(a) Students need to identify that they should tell a potential buyer how much it will cost them to develop the product. (b) Students should identify that good presentations are persuasive.*

ACTIVITY EMBEDDED ASSESSMENT	ACTIVITIES
Collect the following from students after presentations: • Determining Cost Worksheet • Presentation Guidelines Worksheet • Any presentation materials	*Assign Cost to Sunscreen Products* **Say:** The first part of today we will return to our sunscreen products and determine the cost of the sunscreens. Using this worksheet, I want you to calculate the cost to make your sunscreen. This is important information to share with the researchers at Purdue, and you will need to design your marketing campaign around why they should invest in your product. *You might want to elaborate here about how sunscreen formulas that are more expensive to make will need to be especially persuasive to potential investors.* **Hand out Determining Cost Worksheet** (see below) to students. Go over directions and example. Give students 10–15 minutes to use the Cost Sheet to determine how much it will cost to make their sunscreen. Remind them they will turn in one completed copy to you. *Design and Practice Presentations* When students have finished calculating the cost of their sunscreens and completed the follow-up questions, hand out the Presentation Guidelines Worksheet (see below) and the Presentation Rubric (see table 4.14 below) you will be using to assess the presentations. Go over directions for presentations and rubric with students and allow the rest of class period and the following class period for students to design and practice their presentations. Remind them that you will collect one completed Presentation Guidelines Worksheet from each group. *Consider allowing groups to work in the hall or alternative spaces if you feel it is appropriate.* As students are practicing, you should be circulating, answering questions, observing student groups, and providing feedback. *Conduct Presentations* Have students conduct their presentations in front of the whole class. While groups are presenting, have students fill out their Presentation Evaluation page to evaluate each group's sunscreen design and marketing techniques. You can either have students send these over to the group after their presentation, or have students turn them in to you.

	When presentations are complete, have students turn in all presentation materials, one copy of Presentation Guidelines Worksheet, and one copy of Determining Cost Worksheet from each group. *Review Before Post-Unit Test* With any remaining time after presentations, conduct a whole class review session with students prior to conducting the unit post-test. You should go over the engineering design process, the cell cycle, and how errors in the cell cycle can lead to cancer.
POST-ACTIVITY ASSESSMENT	**CLOSURE**
Post-unit test.	Congratulate students on the completion of their projects. Have them turn in all materials to you. Then give post-unit test.
ASSESSMENTS CONTINUED	
N/A	
EDUCATOR RESOURCES	
N/A	

DETERMINING COST WORKSHEET

DIRECTIONS: Use this page to determine the cost of your sunscreen formula to a potential investor. Then discuss and answer the follow-up questions below.

FILL IN THE CHART: Use the information from your **final** sunscreen design, then use the **Cost Sheet** to determine your cost. Make sure you account for the amount of each material you used in your formula. A short example is provided for you.

$$\text{Shea butter} = 0.9 \text{ cents for } 1 \text{ mL}$$
$$\text{You used 3 mL}$$
$$3 \times 0.9 = 2.7 \text{ cents}$$

FOLLOW-UP QUESTIONS

1. Calculate the cost in dollars to produce 50 mL of your sunscreen: _____

2. Use the information below to compare the cost of your sunscreen to the cost of these brands.

BRAND	COST FOR 50 ML
Banana Boat Sport	$2.95
Australia Gold	$1.69
Neutrogena Clear Face	$4.50
Aveeno Baby Sunscreen	$5.91

How does your sunscreen compare? Is it more or less expensive?

3. Based on this information, the information on why you chose your materials, and what you know about mitosis and cancer, why should researchers at Purdue should choose your formula to investigate further? Write a paragraph (4–7 sentences) to answer this question.

COST SHEET

MATERIAL (AMOUNT)	COST OF MATERIAL (¢)
Base Material	
Olive oil (1 mL)	0.8¢
Castor oil (1 mL)	0.5¢
Shea butter (1 mL)	0.9¢
Coconut oil (1 mL)	1.2¢
Add-Ins	
Aloe (1 drop)	0.3¢
Almond Oil (1 drop)	0.7¢
Beeswax (10 drops)	1.0¢
Peppermint oil (1 drop)	0.5¢
Sesame seed oil (1 drop)	1.1¢
Zinc oxide (1 drop)	1.8¢

PRESENTATION GUIDELINES

DIRECTIONS: Use this page to help prepare for your group presentation. Your presentation to the class will need to be at least 5 minutes long and every group member is required to speak. You should take time to carefully consider and plan what each person will talk about and when.

REMEMBER! Your job is to persuade the audience that your product is the best one for the Purdue researchers.

STEP 1: INTRODUCTION
Good presentations have hooks to get the audience's attention!

How do you plan to get the audience's attention for your project? Think and be creative. Describe below what you and your group members plan to do.

STEP 2: SHARE PRODUCT INFORMATION
Good presentations share the important information while keeping the audience engaged!

Nobody likes information-heavy, boring presentations! Think about what your audience absolutely has to know about your product and how you can communicate that with them. Maybe a funny rhyme about your sunscreen formula?

Fill in the information in the checklist below.

CHECKLIST	TASK	NAME OF GROUP MEMBER(S) RESPONSIBLE	HOW WILL YOU CREATIVELY PRESENT THIS INFORMATION?
☐	Share product formula and <u>why</u> formula was chosen.		
☐	Share product cost and how cost compares to other products.		
☐	Explain how product protects against skin cancer.		
☐	Explain connections of product to cell cycle/mitosis. How does your product help maintain normal function of cells?		

STEP 3: SELL IT!

Good presentations must be persuasive!

Why should the audience be convinced that your product is the best? What techniques might you use to convince the class and researchers that your product is worth their time and money?

> **Tip:** Brainstorm with your group successful commercials and brands. What techniques do they use to get you to buy their products? What attracts you to their products or brands?

Write down some ideas here:

STEP 4: PRACTICE

In failing to prepare, you are preparing to fail.

—BENJAMIN FRANKLIN

Take time to practice your presentation with your group. Your presentation needs to last <u>at least 5 minutes</u> and <u>everyone must speak at least once.</u>

Consider using the rubric to score your presentation yourself after you finish practicing one or two times.

STEP 5: FINAL CHECKLIST

Be certain your group has completed the following tasks for your presentation. If tasks are missing, go back and add them.

- Our presentation has a creative hook to get the audience's attention.
- We share our sunscreen formula AND why we chose this formula in our presentation.
- We share the cost of our sunscreen AND how this cost compares to other products in our presentation.
- We share how our product will prevent skin cancer.
- We share how our product connects to the cell cycle and mitosis.
- We try to persuade our audience.
- We explain why our product is the best.

- We have completed our Determining Cost Worksheet.
- We have completed our Presentation Guidelines Worksheet and practiced our presentation.

PRESENTATION EVALUATION

DIRECTIONS: Complete this page to provide feedback for each group as they complete their presentation.

Remember! While feedback is important, it is not nice or fair to be overly critical of one individual or group. Your comments should offer appropriate suggestions for groups to improve their presentation skills.

Dear _____:
(List group members)

Finish these sentences in your own words:
1. I really liked that your group _____.
2. I thought it was interesting when your group said _____.
3. I wish your group would have said more about _____.
4. I will remember _____ about this presentation.

Positives of the presentation:

Changes you would suggest to the group:

In conclusion, I would like to say _____.

_____
(Your name here)

TABLE 4.14. *Designing Sunscreen Unit, Lesson 5, Presentation Rubric*

ASPECT		1	3	5
Presentation	Presentation hook	Minimal or no attempt to engage the audience. Students do not go beyond introducing themselves or stating their names or group name. It is not necessarily clear what the presentation will be about.	Adequate attempt at grabbing audience's attention with short introduction to project. Introduction is appropriate. It is clear what the presentation will be about.	Excellent example of a hook to gain audience's attention. Introduction is appropriate, entertaining, and clearly outlines the presentation's purpose and flow.
	Sunscreen formula	Students provide little to no details about their formula. They do not elaborate on material choices about formula.	Students provide the details of the formula; however, it is not clear the amounts they used or why they chose those materials.	Students provide all the details necessary for their formula and a clear rationale for why they chose all of the materials.
	Sunscreen cost	Students do not share the cost of producing their sunscreen. They do not attempt to relate its cost to other products.	Students share the cost of producing the sunscreen and there are some attempts to compare it to other sunscreen products.	Students share the cost of their product and compare and contrast it to more than one other sunscreen product.
	Connections to the cell cycle	Students make little to no connection between the sunscreen product and the cell cycle.	Students make some connections to the cell cycle, but they may be incomplete or contain inaccuracies.	Students make clear and accurate connections to the cell cycle, explaining how their product will affect cells in the cell cycle.
	Cancer	Students make little to no connection to how their product will prevent skin cancer.	Students attempt to make some connection to how their product will prevent cancer.	Students make thorough and accurate connections to how their product will prevent skin cancer.
	Use of persuasion	Group makes little to no attempt to persuade audience of product.	Group makes reasonable attempt to persuade audience of product but did not succeed, or did not seem fully invested in product themselves. Persuasive techniques are either logical or emotional.	Group succeeds in persuading audience that their product is the best and they are invested in their product. Group's use of persuasion is both logical and emotional.

Determining Cost Worksheet		Worksheet is somewhat complete, but missing answers to follow-up questions, or answers are highly inadequate.	Worksheet is complete but minimally done. Responses are minimal and lack depth.	Worksheet is well done and complete. Answers are of high quality, demonstrating critical thinking skills.
Presentation Guidelines Worksheet		Worksheet is somewhat complete, but missing answers to follow-up questions, or answers are highly inadequate. Demonstrates little to no preparation for presentation.	Worksheet is complete but minimally done. Answers reflect the minimum amount of work to answer the questions and prepare for presentation.	Worksheet is well done and complete. Answers are of high quality, demonstrating critical thinking skills and adequate preparation for presentations.
Group behavior		Few group members were an active part of the presentation. Few group members were well-behaved during the presentation. Group members did not give feedback to other presentation groups.	Most group members were an active part of the presentation. Most group members were well-behaved during the presentation. Group members provided some feedback to other groups during presentations but inconsistently.	All group members were an active part of the presentation. All group members were well-behaved during the presentation and provided feedback to other groups on Presentation Evaluation pages.
			Team Score	/45

Note: An earlier version of this rubric was published elsewhere (Bogan and Guzey 2023).

5

ADVANCING INTEGRATED STEM EDUCATION: FUTURE DIRECTIONS AND RESEARCH OPPORTUNITIES

Research has shown the benefits of integrated STEM education for teachers and students. However, there is still much to learn about meaningful, purposeful, and effective integrated STEM education. This chapter outlines several directions for future research.

Early research and program development in integrated STEM education largely focused on elementary education. Numerous curriculum materials were created to help elementary teachers integrate two or more STEM subjects using interdisciplinary approaches. Some of these curriculum materials also incorporated elements from the arts, literacy, or computer science (Tank et al. 2013). These efforts were particularly successful since elementary teachers typically have greater flexibility to teach across disciplines. As a result, many integrated STEM units reached a wide range of elementary classrooms. However, fewer resources have been available for secondary teachers. At the middle and high school levels, implementing integrated STEM approaches presents unique challenges and often requires collaboration among teachers from different subject areas. For example, a biology teacher may need to coordinate with mathematics and engineering teachers to deliver a unit in which students learn concepts from multiple disciplines and apply them to a design challenge. To advance integrated education at the secondary level, future research should explore strategies to support secondary teachers in adopting integrated approaches. Additionally, studies are needed to examine the design and impact of instructional materials developed for integrated STEM instruction tailored to this context.

Although many studies have explored the integration of engineering design and content in the K–12 science curriculum, much of this work has concentrated on physical sciences. In contrast, relatively few studies have focused on such integration with the life sciences curriculum (e.g., Guzey 2017; Lachapelle et al. 2011). Engineering design can enhance students' understanding of many biological concepts by engaging students in real-world design challenges, such as designing medical devices or solutions for wastewater treatment. Expanding research in this area could provide valuable insights into how engineering design enhances life science education.

Another underexplored area is the development of assessments that align with integrated STEM instruction. Traditional assessments are often inadequate in measuring student learning in classrooms where students engage in interdisciplinary instruction (Douglas et al. 2020). The majority of curriculum materials developed for integrated STEM instruction have students design experiments, collect and analyze data, engage in engineering design process, and apply knowledge from science and/or math to solve engineering design challenges. There is a need for assessment tools that capture students' content knowledge or skill development and application of concepts in authentic, integrated contexts.

Finally, while much of the existing integrated STEM education research has focused on the impact of instructional materials or professional development programs on teachers and/or students, the sustainability of STEM initiatives remains an overlooked area. Many school districts create STEM initiatives and offer professional development programs for teachers. The long-term success of these programs depends on sustained funding and support. Sustained funding is a big challenge for many school districts. Additionally, short-term efforts or programs that do not fully support teachers in adopting new practices often have limited impact on teachers or students. Future studies should investigate the design, delivery, and structural elements of successful, sustainable programs to inform long-term implementation strategies.

CONCLUSION: REFLECTIONS AND IMPLICATIONS FOR PRACTICE AND POLICY

This book is a resource for educators, researchers, and policymakers who are committed to advancing integrated STEM education. Through a review of the literature, it offers a clear understanding of the impact of integrated STEM education on teachers' teaching practices and student outcomes. The framework and instructional guide included in this book offer practical tools and can be used to develop new curricular materials. The sample units provide step-by-step guidance for lesson implementation and offer suggestions for guiding students as they engage in engineering design to solve design solutions. Additionally, the final chapter outlines suggestions and directions for future research that are essential for the advancement of integrated STEM education.

For a broad and widespread implementation of integrated STEM education approaches, educators need to have access to resources including curriculum materials. Curriculum resources are most effective and impactful when they are developed from evidence-based or research-based practices and build on theories of teaching and learning, which demonstrates the need for and importance of research in integrated STEM education. Robust research allows for bridging the theory and practice and provides guidance in advancing STEM teaching and learning in K–12 classrooms and beyond.

As discussed throughout this book, integrated STEM education can take many forms. The approach presented herein, which was developed specifically for and tested in middle school science classrooms, offers one effective model for integrating science and engineering. However, a variety of strategies and approaches could support interdisciplinary teaching across a range of subjects and contexts. Regardless of the discipline or setting, teachers need support as they plan and implement integrated instructional approaches. School and district administrators, policymakers, and educators must work together to create learning environments that foster interdisciplinary learning. This could include aligning education standards, providing time for collaborative planning, establishing professional learning communities, offering targeted professional development programs, or providing funding support for materials and equipment needed for design activities that support teachers and enrich student learning.

Ultimately, creating, implementing, and studying meaningful and engaging learning experiences for integrated STEM education are essential for better preparing students to succeed in an increasingly competitive, technology-driven world.

REFERENCES

Anwar, Saira, Muhsin Menekse, Siddika Selcen Guzey, and Lynn A. Bryan. 2022. "The Effectiveness of an Integrated STEM Curriculum Unit on Middle School Students' Life Science Learning." *Journal of Research in Science Teaching* 59 (7): 1204–34. https://doi.org/10.1002/tea.21756.

Atman, Cynthia J., Robin S. Adams, Monica E. Cardella, Jennifer Turns, Susan Mosborg, and Jason Saleem. 2007. "Engineering Design Processes: A Comparison of Students and Expert Practitioners." *Journal of Engineering Education* 96 (4): 359–79. https://doi.org/10.1002/j.2168-9830.2007.tb00945.x.

Berland, Leema K., and Rebecca Steingut. 2016. "Explaining Variation in Student Efforts Towards Using Math and Science Knowledge in Engineering Contexts." *International Journal of Science Education* 38 (18): 2742–61. https://doi.org/10.1080/09500693.2016.1260179.

Bogan, Valarie, and S. Selcen Guzey. 2023. "Case: Sunscreen Design for Assessing Students' Engineering Practices and Science Learning." In *Navigating Elementary Science Teaching and Learning*, edited by Sophia Jeong, Lynn A. Bryan, Deborah J. Tippins, and Chelsea M. Sexton. Springer.

Brophy, Sean, Stacy Klein, Merredith Portsmore, and Chris Rogers. 2008. "Advancing Engineering Education in P-12 Classrooms." *Journal of Engineering Education* 97 (3): 369–87. https://doi.org/10.1002/j.2168-9830.2008.tb00985.x.

Calabrese Barton, Angela, Hosun Kang, Edna Tan, Tara B. O'Neill, Juanita Bautista-Guerra, and Caitlin Brecklin. 2013. "Crafting a Future in Science: Tracing Middle School Girls' Identity Work Over Time and Space." *American Educational Research Journal* 50 (1): 37–75. https://doi.org/10.3102/0002831212458142

Calabrese Barton, Angela, Edna Tan, and Day Greenberg. 2017. "The Makerspace Movement: Sites of Possibilities for Equitable Opportunities to Engage Underrepresented Youth in STEM." *Teachers College Record* 119 (6): 1–44. https://doi.org/10.1177/016146811711900608.

Capobianco, Brenda M., and James Lehman. 2018. "Examining and Characterizing Elementary School Teachers' Engineering Design-Based Instructional Practices and Their Impact on Students' Science Achievement." Paper presented at 2018 ASEE Annual Conference & Exposition, Salt Lake City, UT, June 23, 2018. https://peer.asee.org/30465.

Carlson, Lawrence E., and Jacquelyn F. Sullivan. 2004. "Exploiting Design to Inspire Interest in Engineering Across the K-16 Engineering Curriculum." *International Journal of Engineering Education* 20 (3): 372–80.

Chin, Christine, and Li-Gek Chia. 2006. "Problem-Based Learning: Using Ill-Structured Problems in Biology Project Work." *Science Education* 90 (1): 44–67. https://doi.org/10.1002/sce.20097.

Crismond, David P., and Robin S. Adams. 2012. "The Informed Design Teaching and Learning Matrix." *Journal of Engineering Education* 101 (4): 738–97. https://doi.org/10.1002/j.2168-9830.2012.tb01127.x.

Crotty, Elizabeth A., Selcen S. Guzey, Gillian H. Roehrig, Aran W. Glancy, Elizabeth A. Ring-Whalen, and Tamara J. Moore. 2017. "Approaches to Integrating Engineering in STEM Units and Student Achievement Gains." *Journal of Pre-College Engineering Education Research* 7 (2): Article 1. https://doi.org/10.7771/2157-9288.1148.

Cunningham, Christine M., and Gregory J. Kelly. 2017. "Epistemic Practices of Engineering for Education." *Science Education* 101 (3): 486–505. https://doi.org/10.1002/sce.21271.

Cunningham, Christine M., and Cathy P. Lachapelle. 2014. "Designing Engineering Experiences to Engage All Students." In *Engineering in Pre-College Settings: Synthesizing Research, Policy, and Practices*, edited by Şenay Purzer, Johannes Strobel, and Monica E. Cardella. Purdue University Press.

Cunningham, Christine M., Cathy P. Lachapelle, Robert T. Brennan, Gregory J. Kelly, Chris San Antonio Tunis, and Christine A. Gentry. 2020. "The Impact of Engineering Curriculum Design Principles on Elementary Students' Engineering and Science Learning." *Journal of Research in Science Teaching* 57 (3): 423–53. https://doi.org/10.1002/tea.21601.

Dare, Emily A., Joshua A. Ellis, and Gillian H. Roehrig. 2014. "Driven by Beliefs: Understanding Challenges Physical Science Teachers Face When Integrating Engineering and Physics." *Journal of Pre-College Engineering Education Research* 4 (2): Article 5. https://doi.org/10.7771/2157-9288.1098.

Dare, Emily A., Joshua A. Ellis, and Gillian H. Roehrig. 2018. "Understanding Science Teachers' Implementations of Integrated STEM Curricular Units Through a Phenomenological Multiple Case Study." *International Journal of STEM Education* 5 (February): Article 4. https://doi.org/10.1186/s40594-018-0101-z.

Desy, Elizabeth A., Scott A. Peterson, and Vicky Brockman. 2011. "Gender Differences in Science-Related Attitudes and Interests Among Middle School and High School Students." *Science Educator* 20 (2): 23–30.

Dorst, Kees. "The Core of Design Thinking and Its Applications." 2011. *Design Studies* 32 (6): 521–32. https://doi.org/10.1016/j.destud.2011.07.006.

Douglas, K., Brian D. Gane, Knut Neumann, and James W. Pellegrino. 2020. "Contemporary Methods of Assessing Integrated STEM Competencies." In *Handbook of Research on STEM Education*, edited by Carla C. Johnson, Margaret J. Mohr-Schroeder, Tamara J. Moore, and Lyn D. English. Routledge.

Dym, Clive L., Alice M. Agogino, Ozgur Eris, Daniel D. Frey, and Larry J. Leifer. 2005. "Engineering Design Thinking, Teaching, and Learning." *Journal of Engineering Education* 94 (1): 103–20. https://doi.org/10.1002/j.2168-9830.2005.tb00832.x.

English, Lyn D., and Donna King 2019. "STEM Integration in Sixth Grade: Designing and Constructing Paper Bridges." *International Journal of Science and Mathematics Education* 17 (June): 863–84. https://doi.org/10.1007/s10763-018-9912-0.

English, Lyn D., Donna King, and Joanna Smeed. 2017. "Advancing Integrated STEM Learning Through Engineering Design: Sixth-Grade Students' Design and Construction of Earthquake Resistant Buildings." *The Journal of Educational Research* 110 (3): 255–71. https://doi.org/10.1080/00220671.2016.1264053.

Fortus, David, R. Charles Dershimer, Joseph Krajcik, Ronald W. Marx, and Rachel Mamlok-Naaman. 2004. "Design-Based Science and Student Learning." *Journal of Research in Science Teaching* 41 (10): 1081–110. https://doi.org/10.1002/tea.20040.

Ganesh, Tirupalavanam G., and Christine G. Schnittka. 2014. "Engineering Education in the Middle Grades." In *Engineering in Pre-College Settings: Synthesizing Research, Policy, and Practices*, edited by Şenay Purzer, Johannes Strobel, and Monica E. Cardella. Purdue University Press.

García-Carmona, Antonio, Granada Muñoz-Franco, and Marta Cruz-Guzmán. 2025. "Integration of Engineering Practices into Primary Science Classrooms." *Science & Education*. https://doi.org/10.1007/s11191-025-00616-5.

Government of Canada. (2014). *Seizing Canada's Moment: Moving Forward in Science, Technology, and Innovation 2014*. https://ised-isde.canada.ca/site/plans-reports/sites/default/files/attachments/Seizing_Moment_ST_I-Report-2014-eng.pdf

Grossman, Jennifer M., and Michelle V. Porche. 2014. "Perceived Gender and Racial/Ethnic Barriers to STEM Success." *Urban Education* 49 (6): 698–727. https://doi.org/10.1177/0042085913481364.

Guzey, S. Selcen, Michael Harwell, Mario Moreno, Yadira Peralta, and Tamara Moore. 2017. "The Impact of Design-Based STEM Integration Curricula on Student Achievement in Engineering, Science, and Mathematics." *Journal of Science Education and Technology* 26 (2): 207–22. https://doi.org/10.1007/s10956-016-9673-x.

Guzey, S. Selcen, and Weiling Li. 2023. "A Longitudinal Study of Middle School Students' Science Learning in the Context of Integrated STEM Instruction." *Journal of Science Education and Technology* 32 (2): 168–80. https://doi.org/10.1007/s10956-022-10023-y.

Guzey, S. Selcen, Tamara J. Moore, and Gillian Morse. 2016. "Student Interest in Engineering Design-Based Science." *School Science and Mathematics* 116 (8): 409–60. https://doi.org/10.1111/ssm.12198.

Guzey, S. Selcen, Elizabeth A. Ring-Whalen, Michael Harwell, and Yadira Peralta. 2019. "Life STEM: A Case Study of Life Science Learning Through Engineering Design." *International Journal of Science and Mathematics Education* 17 (January): 23–42. https://doi.org/10.1007/s10763-017-9860-0.

Guzey, S. Selcen, Kristina Tank, Hui-Hui Wang, Gillian Roehrig, and Tamara Moore. 2014. "A High-Quality Professional Development for Teachers of Grades 3–6 for Implementing Engineering into Classrooms." *School Science and Mathematics* 114 (3): 139–49. https://doi.org/10.1111/ssm.12061.

Halawa, Suarman, Ying Shao Hsu, Wen Xin Zhang, Yen Ruey Kuo, and Jen Yi Wu. 2020. "Features and Trends of Teaching Strategies for Scientific Practices from a Review of 2008–2017 Articles." *International Journal of Science Education* 42 (7): 1183–1206. https://doi.org/10.1080/09500693.2020.1752415.

Halawa, Suarman, Tzu-Chiang Lin, and Ying-Shao Hsu. 2024. "Exploring Instructional Design in K-12 STEM Education: A Systematic Literature Review." *Internaltional Journal of STEM Ed* 11, Article 43. https://doi.org/10.1186/s40594-024-00503-5.

Hiwatig, Benny Mart R., Gillian H. Roehrig, and Mark D. Rouleau. 2024. "Unpacking the Nuances: An Exploratory Multilevel Analysis on the Operationalization of Integrated STEM Education and Student Attitudinal Change." *Disciplinary and Interdisciplinary Science Education Research* 6, Article 18. https://doi.org/10.1186/s43031-024-00108-6.

Kelley, Todd R., and J. Geoff Knowles. 2016. "A Conceptual Framework for Integrated STEM Education." *International Journal of STEM Education*, 3, Article 11, https://doi.org/10.1186/s40594-016-0046-z.

Keratithamkul, Khomson, Justine N. Kim, and Gillian H. Roehrig. 2020. "Cultural Competence or Deficit-Based View? A Qualitative Approach to Understanding Middle School Students' Experience with Culturally Framed Engineering." *International Journal of STEM Education*, 7, Article 26. https://doi.org/10.1186/s40594-020-00224-5.

King, Natalie S., and Rose M. Pringle. 2019. "Black Girls Speak STEM: Counterstories of Informal and Formal Learning Experiences." *Journal of Research in Science Teaching* 56 (5): 539–69.

Lachapelle, Cathy P., Jocz, Jennifer, and Phadnis, Preeya. 2011. *Engineering Is Elementary: An Evaluation of Years 4 Through 6 Field Testing*. Museum of Science, Boston.

Li, Yeping, Ke Wang, Yu Xiao, and Jeffrey E. Froyd. 2020. "Research and Trends in STEM Education: A Systematic Review of Journal Publications." *International Journal of STEM Education* 7, Article 11. https://doi.org/10.1186/s40594-020-00207-6.

McLure, Felicity I., Kok-Sing Tang, and P. John Williams. 2022. "What Do Integrated STEM Projects Look Like in Middle School and High School Classrooms? A Systematic Literature Review of Empirical Studies of iSTEM Projects." *International Journal of STEM Education* 9, Article 73. https://doi.org/10.1186/s40594-022-00390-8.

Mehalik, Matthew M., Yaron Doppelt, and Christian D. Schuun. 2008. "Middle-School Science Through Design-Based Learning Versus Scripted Inquiry: Better Overall Science Concept Learning." *Journal of Engineering Education* 97 (January): 71–85. https://doi.org/10.1002/j.2168-9830.2008.tb00955.x.

Mentzer, Nathan, Kurt Becker, and Mathias Sutton. "Engineering Design Thinking: High School Students' Performance and Knowledge." 2015. *Journal of Engineering Education* 104 (4): 417–32. https://doi.org/10.1002/jee.20105.

Minner, Daphne D., Abigail Jurist Levy, and Jeanne Century. 2010. "Inquiry-Based Instruction: What Is It and Does It Matter? Results from a Research Synthesis Years 1984 to 2002." *Journal of Research in Science Teaching* 47 (4): 474–96. https://doi.org/10.1002/tea.20347.

Mitchell, Mathew. 1993. "Situational Interest: Its Multifaceted Structure in the Secondary School Mathematics Classroom." *Journal of Educational Psychology* 85 (3): 424–36. https://doi.org/10.1037/0022-0663.85.3.424.

Moore, T., Amanda C. Johnston, and Aran W. Glancy. 2020. "STEM Integration: A Synthesis of Conceptual Frameworks and Definitions." In *Handbook on Research in STEM Education*, edited by Carla C. Johnson, Margaret J. Mohr-Schroeder, Tamara J. Moore, and Lyn D. English. Routledge.

Moore, Tamara J., Micah S. Stohlmann, Hui-Hui Wang, Kristina M. Tank, Aran W. Glancy, and Gillian H. Roehrig. 2014. "Implementation and Integration of Engineering in K–12 STEM Education." In *Engineering in Pre-College Settings: Synthesizing Research, Policy, and Practices*, edited by Şenay Purzer, Johannes Strobel, and Monica E. Cardella. Purdue University Press.

National Academies of Sciences, Engineering, and Medicine (NASEM). 2019. *Science and Engineering for Grades 6–12: Investigation and Design at the Center*. National Academies Press. https://doi.org/10.17226/25216.

National Academies of Sciences, Engineering, and Medicine (NASEM). 2020. *Building Capacity for Teaching Engineering in K–12 Education*. National Academies Press. https://doi.org/10.17226/25612.

National Research Council (NRC). 2010. *Exploring the Intersection of Science Education and 21st Century Skills: A Workshop Summary*. National Academies Press.

National Research Council (NRC). 2012. *A Framework for K–12 Science Education: Practices, Crosscutting Concepts, and Core Ideas*. National Academies Press.

NGSS Lead States. 2013. *Next Generation Science Standards: For States, By States*. National Academies Press. https://doi.org/10.17226/13165.

Office of the Chief Scientist. 2014. *Science, Technology, Engineering and Mathematics: Australia's Future*. Australian Government, Canberra. https://www.chiefscientist.gov.au/sites/default/files/STEM_AustraliasFuture_Sept2014_Web.pdf.

Pleasant, Jacob, and Joanne K. Olson. 2019. "What Is Engineering? Elaborating the Nature of Engineering for K–12 Education." *Science Education* 103 (1): 145–66. https://doi.org/10.1002/sce.21483.

Ring-Whalen, E., Emily A. Dare, Elizabeth A. Crotty, and Gillian H. Roehrig. 2017. "The Evolution of Teacher Conceptions of STEM Education Throughout an Intensive Professional Development Experience." *Journal of Science Teacher Education* 28 (5): 444–67. https://doi.org/10.1080/1046560X.2017.1356671.

Ring-Whalen, Elizabeth, Emily Dare, Gillian Roehrig, Preethi Titu, and Elizabeth Crotty. 2018. "From Conception to Curricula: The Role of Science, Technology, Engineering, and Mathematics in Integrated STEM Units." *International Journal of Education in Mathematics, Science and Technology* 6 (4): 343–62. https://digitalcommons.mtu.edu/michigantech-p/13685/.

Riskowski, Jody L., Carrie Davis Todd, Bryan Wee, Melissa Dark, and Jon Harbor. 2009. "Exploring the Effectiveness of an Interdisciplinary Water Resources Engineering Module in an Eighth Grade Science Course." *International Journal of Engineering Education* 25 (1): 181–95. https://www.ijee.ie/articles/Vol25-1/s22_Ijee2125.pdf.

Roehrig, Gillian H., Emily A. Dare, Joshua A. Ellis, and Elizabeth Ring-Whalen. 2021. "Beyond the Basics: A Detailed Conceptual Framework of Integrated STEM." *Disciplinary and Interdisciplinary Science Education Research* 3, Article 11. https://doi.org/10.1186/s43031-021-00041-y.

Siverling, Emilie A., Tamara J. Moore, Elizabeth Suazo-Flores, Corey A. Mathis, and S. Selcen Guzey. 2021. "What Initiates Evidence-Based Reasoning? Situations That Prompt Students to Support Their Design Ideas and Decisions." *Journal of Engineering Education* 110 (2): 294–317. https://doi.org/10.1002/jee.20384.

Tank, Kristina, Christy Pettis, Tamara Moore, and Abby Fehr. 2013. "Hamsters, Picture Books, and Engineering Design: A STEM Unit Teaches Primary Students about Engineering Design." *Science and Children* 50 (9): 59–63. https://doi.org/10.2505/4/sc13_050_09_59.

Valtorta, Clara G., and Leema K. Berland. 2015. "Math, Science, and Engineering Integration in a High School Engineering Course: A Qualitative Study." *Journal of Pre-College Engineering Education Research (J-PEER)* 5 (1): Article 3. https://doi.org/10.7771/2157-9288.1087.

Wendell, Kristen B., and Chris Rogers. 2013. "Engineering Design-Based Science, Science Content Performance, and Science Attitudes in Elementary School." *Journal of Engineering Education* 102 (4): 513–40. https://doi.org/10.1002/jee.20026.

Wendell, Kristen B., Christopher G. Wright, and Patricia Paugh. 2017. "Reflective Decision-Making in Elementary Students' Engineering Design." *Journal of Engineering Education* 106 (3): 356–97. https://doi.org/10.1002/jee.20173.

Wiggins, Grant, and Jay McTighe. 2005. *Understanding by Design*, 2nd ed. Pearson.

Wilson-Lopez, Amy, and Angela Minichiello. 2017. "Disciplinary Literacy in Engineering." *Journal of Adolescent & Adult Literacy* 61 (1): 7–14. https://doi.org/10.1002/jaal.658.

Wilson-Lopez, Amy, Ashley R. Strong, Christina M. Hartman, Jared Garlick, Karen H. Washburn, Angela Minichiello, Sandra Weingart, and Jorge Acosta-Feliz. 2020. "A Systematic Review of Argumentation Related to the Engineering-Designed World." *Journal of Engineering Education* 109 (2): 281–306. https://doi.org/10.1002/jee.20318.

Zhou, Shuqi, Zehua Dong, Hui Hui Wang, and Ming Ming Chiu. 2024. "A Meta-Analysis of STEM Integration on Student Academic Achievement." *Research in Science Education* (December). https://doi.org/10.1007/s11165-024-10216-y.

ABOUT THE AUTHOR

S. SELCEN GUZEY is a professor of science education in the Department of Curriculum and Instruction in the College of Education at Purdue University. Her research and teaching focus on integrated STEM education, with particular emphasis on supporting K–12 science teachers in bringing engineering into the classroom. Guzey has created numerous curriculum materials and led professional development programs to help teachers implement interdisciplinary STEM instruction.

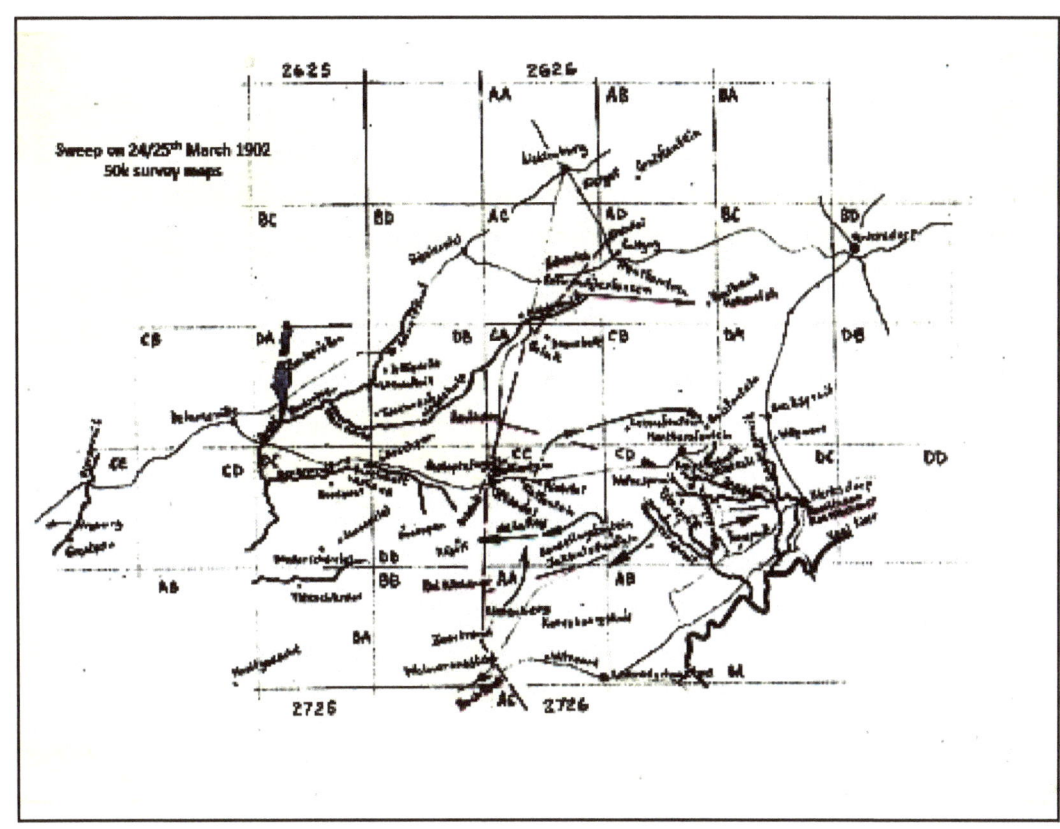

Sweep on 31 March/1 April 1902
Battle of Boschbult
50k survey maps.

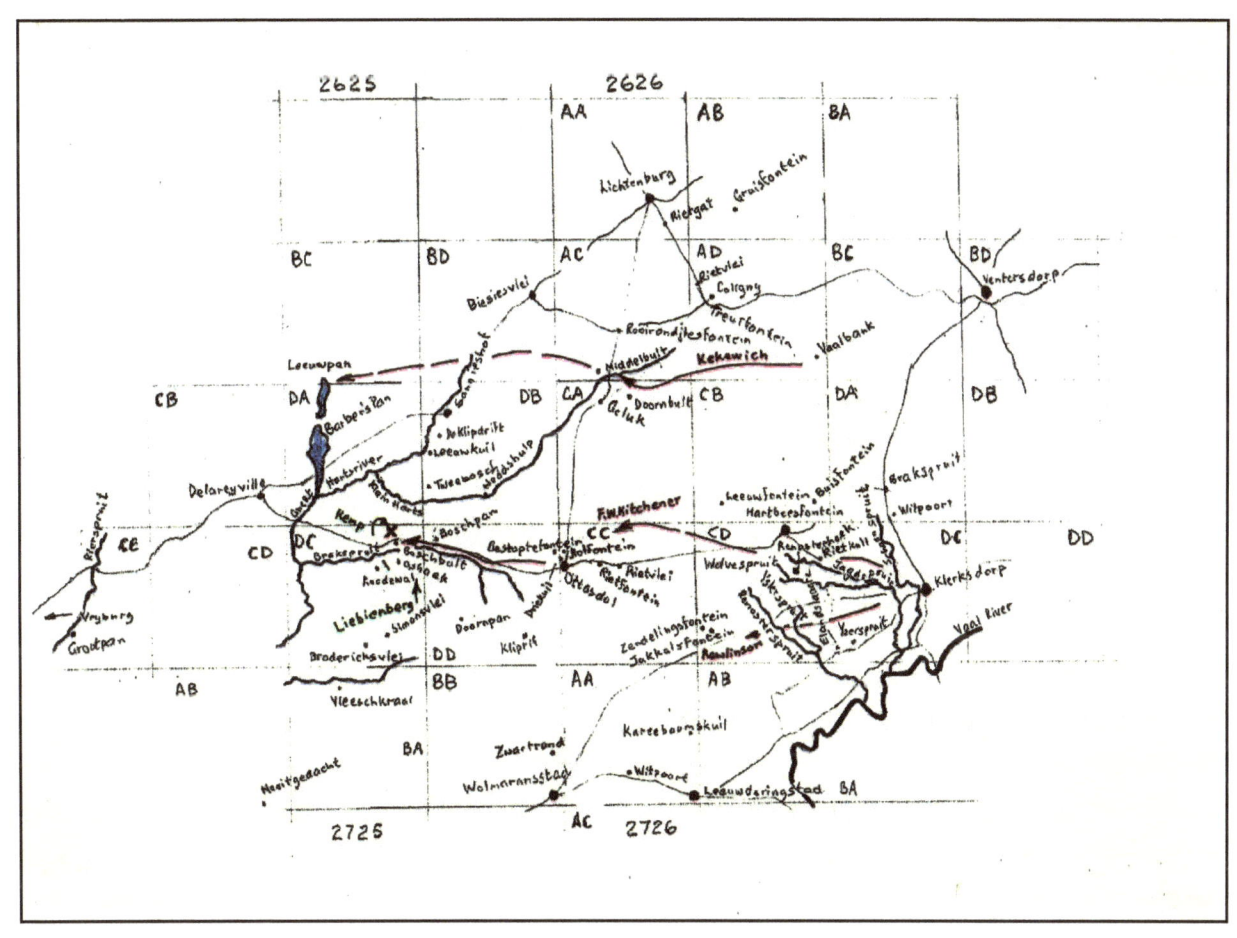

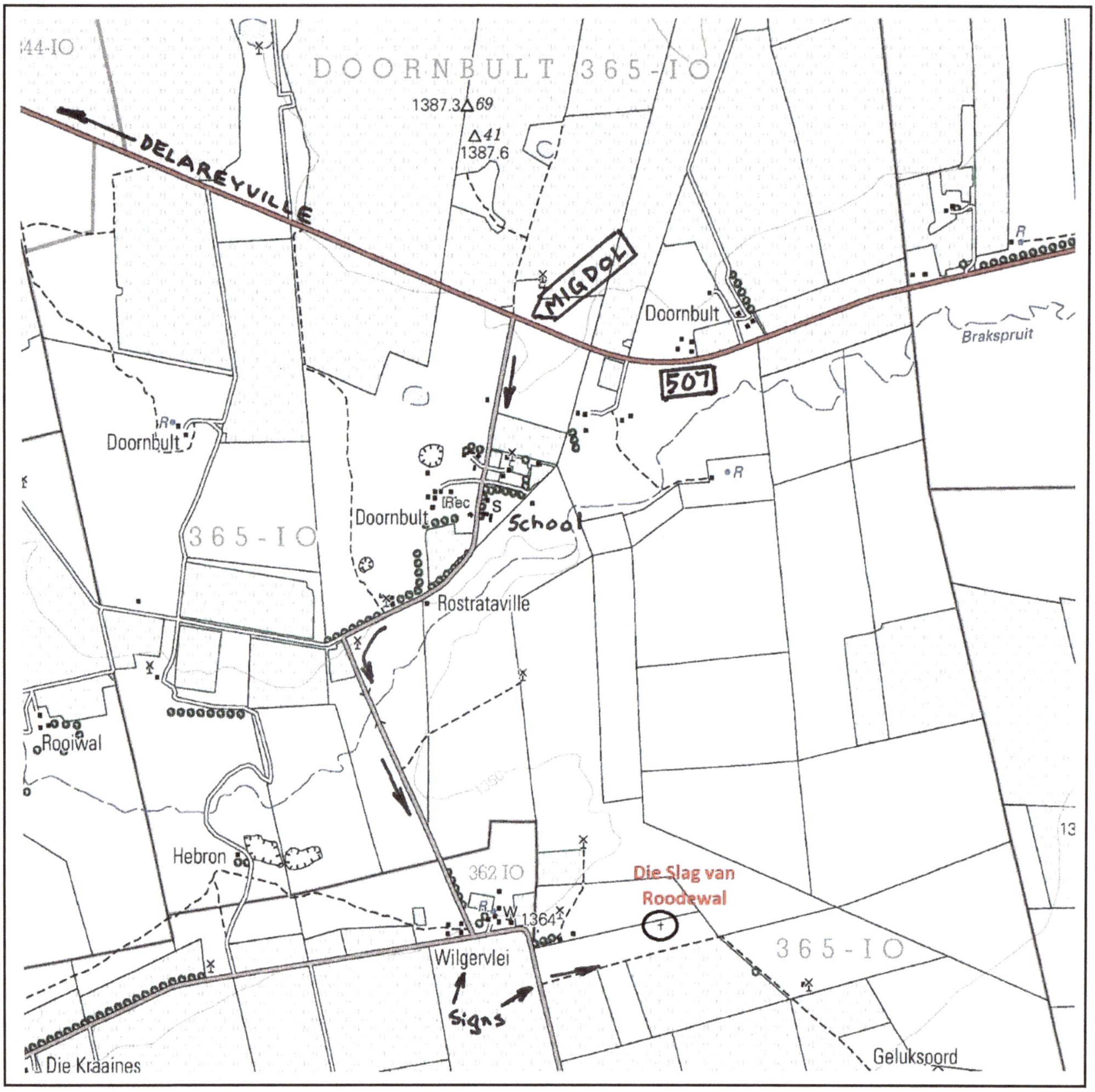

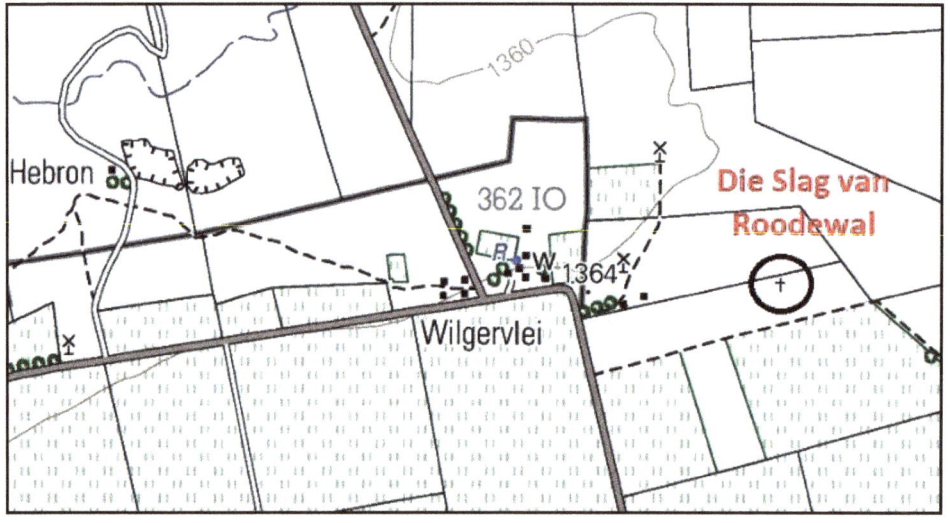

Roodewal battle site and monument.

The grave of Lieutenant G.H.B. Coulson D.S.O. V.C. on Lambrechtsfontein, in need of repair.

Directions to Lambrechtsfontein:
(The tarred road is R59 about 19kms south of Bothaville.)
Turn to Kommandodrif.
Turn right onto S1034.
After 8kms turn left onto Lambrechtsfontein farm.

Lambrechtsfontein: The re-dedication ceremony with the men of the Wit Rifles Regiment.

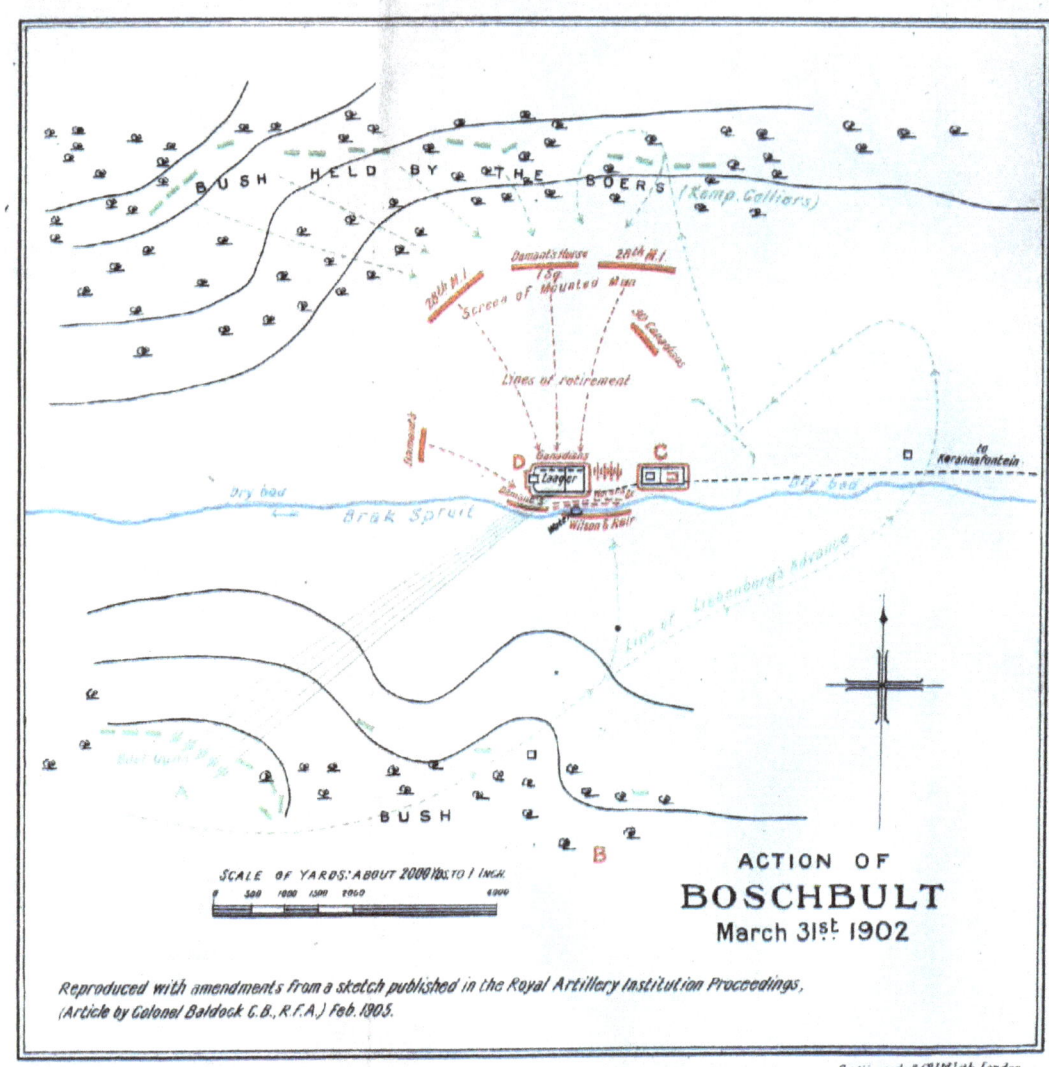

RIFLE AND SPADE.
Cookson's force entrenching to meet the onset of Kemp.

TER
NAGEDACHTENIS VAN
WIJLE KOMMANDANT
FERDINAND JACOBUS
POTGIETER
EN 'N VEERTIGTAL ANDER
HELDE GESNEUWELD OP
11 APRIL 1902
VIR VOLK EN VADERLAND.
OPGERIG 11 APRIL 1921 A.D.

Roodewal

Tweebosch / Klipspruit

BURGERS GESNEUWEL TE DE KLIPDRIFT
7 MAART 1902
SLAG VAN METHUEN

- VKT HENDRIK P. ERASMUS
- BGRS. IGNATIUS S. BADENHORST
- PIET BILL
- PETRUS P. ERASMUS
- ROELOF ESTERHUIZEN
- MARTHINUS S. JOUBERT
- JOHANNES P. LOUW
- WILLEM J. L. PRETORIUS
- SAREL V. D. MERWE

Monument and headstone to General Koos de la Rey.

Beautiful marble monument in the Garden of Remembrance, Treurfontein, Coligny.

AMNESTY DENIED
Salmon van As, Barend Celliers and Josef Muller

The Peace of Vereeniging, 31 May 1902 and the amnesty

Peace in the Anglo-Boer War did not come easily. It seemed to be more difficult to stop the war than to start it. Peace had been a long time coming. Early in February 1901, it seemed that an opportunity for negotiation had arisen. General Louis Botha's night attack at Bothwell (Lake Chrissie) had been beaten off, although Major-General Horace Smith-Dorrien had lost so many horses that pursuit was only half-hearted. General Christiaan de Wet's invasion of the Cape Colony, in company with the Orange Free State President Marthinus Steyn, was also being beaten back.

Mrs Botha, living in Pretoria, was given a letter to send to her husband. A meeting with the British Commander-in-Chief, Lord Kitchener, was proposed for the purpose of arranging terms of peace. Everything was up for discussion "except that the question of independence of the two republics was not to be discussed in any way." This, of course, was Botha's opening gambit when he and Kitchener met at Middelburg on 28 February 1901. Kitchener refused to discuss this point, but, nevertheless, details of a possible settlement were discussed in a friendly and reasonable spirit. After the meeting, a draft letter was sent by British High Commissioner Sir Alfred Milner to the British Government who returned it for Kitchener to send a final version to Botha on 7 March 1901. With Botha's letter of 16 March, the Boers declined to negotiate further (Chilvers Vol V, 1907, p183).

Another year would pass before there was a further development that was to lead eventually to the Peace of Vereeniging. The Boers had sent a three-man deputation to Europe in March 1900, and they had been given full powers to canvass support for the Boer cause but were acknowledged only by the government of the Netherlands. In January 1902, the Dutch Government proposed that they would act as a neutral power to mediate a peace agreement. The Boer peace delegates were to be sent to South Africa to deliberate with their leaders in the field. On their return they would be put "in communication with the British Government and given facilities for the conduct of negotiations in Holland". (The members of this deputation were Abram Fischer, J.B. Wessels and A.D.W. Wolmarans, all executive members of their respective governments).

Intervention by a foreign power was clearly not acceptable to Lord Lansdowne, the British Secretary for War, acting on behalf of the British Government. Nevertheless, Kitchener was empowered to send a copy of all the correspondence relating to this matter to the Transvaal Government, which he did on 7 March 1902 without explanation or comment of any sort.

The Acting President of the Transvaal, Schalk Burger replied that he was "desirous and prepared to make peace proposals" but indicated that he needed to meet President Steyn of the Free State "to enable us to make a proposal jointly" (letter from Acting President Schalk Burger to General Lord Kitchener, 10 March 1902). The Acting President was met at Balmoral Station by a special train and taken to Kroonstad. Kitchener had been sent a telegram from Burger to be forwarded to Steyn, but the British commander responded that "it is...not easy for me to communicate him, especially as he does not at present make a prolonged stay in any part of the country" (letter from General Lord Kitchener to Acting President Schalk Burger, 18 March 1902).

From Kroonstad, two dispatch riders, Robberts and Hattingh, were sent out to find President Steyn. He was with General Koos de la Rey at Zendelingsfontein, west of Klerksdorp, under-going treatment for his eyes by de la Rey's Russian doctor, Gustavus von Rennenhampf (See De Villiers, Vol II, 2008, pp167-170, for details of President Steyn's illness).

Steyn suggested "Klerksorp or Potchefstroom or any farm in that neighbourhood which His Excellency Lord Kitchener may consider most suitable" for a meeting with the Transvaal Government. Klerksdorp was confirmed as the venue and the first meeting took place on 9 April. After three days of discussions, it was agreed that they should meet with Kitchener in Pretoria so as to put forward their proposals and they arrived there on 12 April. Both sides presented their views, the upshot being that the Boers would elect thirty representatives from each of the two republics to meet in Vereeniging to finally negotiate an agreement leading to a cessation of hostilities.

Proceedings began on 15 May 1902 in a large tent outside the town. The discussions were tortuous with so large a number of representatives with widely divergent views. Many considered that they should (and could) fight on for at least another year, but others thought that they had reached the bitter end (Kestell & van Velden, *The Peace Negotiations*, 1912, give full details of the proceedings of the meetings at Klerksdorp, Vereeniging and Pretoria). Finally, a draft peace treaty was telegraphed to the British Government, who responded on 28 May with their proposal.

General Botha asked whether there would be "any objection to the delegates deleting some clause or other from the proposal now submitted by the British Government?" but Lord Milner replied "there can be no alteration, there must simply be a reply of 'yes' or 'no'" (Kestell and van Velden, 1912, p136).

Very broadly, the proposals were much as Kitchener had discussed with Botha the previous year at Middelburg, but codified with clauses for each of the conditions. The surrender of burgher forces, the return of prisoners-of-war and a number of other conditions were laid down in ten clauses with a further statement describing the payment of reparations.

On Thursday, 29 May, the proposals were put to the Boer delegates for them to decide on one of three actions — to continue the struggle, to accept the proposals of the British Government or to surrender unconditionally. After further deliberation, they gave the "yes" reply, albeit reluctantly, meeting the British deadline of midnight on 31 May.

Clause 4 of the proposals read as follows and caused some discussion at Vereeniging as to what was meant or implied: *"No Proceedings, CIVIL or CRIMINAL, will be taken against any of the BURGHERS so surrendering or so returning for any Acts in connection with the prosecution of the War. The benefit of this Clause will not extend to certain Acts contrary to the usages of War which have been notified by the Commander-in-Chief to the Boer Generals, and which shall be tried by Court Martial immediately after the close of hostilities."*

During these final deliberations, General S.P. du Toit of Wolmaransstad asked Botha to clarify the meaning of the clause, asking, "May I know what acts are here referred to?" Botha then notified the meeting that Kitchener had communicated informally to him that the three persons concerned were: *"Mr van Aswegen [sic] for the shooting of Captain Mears [sic]; Mr Celliers for the shooting of Capt Boyle; and a certain Muller for the alleged murder of a certain Rademeyer in the district of Vrede. These three persons will have to stand their trial on the conclusion of peace"* (Kestell & van Velden, 1912, p141). The names of van As and Miers are misspelled.

Kitchener told Botha that these three alleged murders "had attracted much attention in England, and that the British Government...did not see their way open to leave these three cases untried." On a later occasion, Kitchener repeated, in the presence of both Botha and General Smuts, that only these three would be excluded from the benefit of Clause 4. General George Brand, son of former President Sir John Brand of the Orange Free State, asked why these names were not inserted in the peace proposal. General Hertzog explained that the British Governrnent had required that there could be no alterations made.

General Christiaan de Wet was not satisfied with this, saying that they had only the word of Lord Kitchener and that it is not down in black and white, that the three persons mentioned will be the only exceptions. General de la Rey explained that "only the three persons mentioned are excluded...and because we were afraid that there might be more cases, General Botha went and satisfied himself" (Kestell & van Velden, 1912, p142).

At the peace conference, Kitchener told Louis Botha that the British Government required the three alleged murderers to stand trial immediately after the cessation of hostilities. It appears that the Boer leaders had little option but to agree to terms which made provision for the three burghers to stand trial. Conceivably they did this so as to avoid any more burghers being prosecuted for "crimes against the usages of war". Shortly after the conclusion of the peace, Salmon van As was tried and executed, even though Botha had assured him that nothing would happen to him. Louis Slabbert, who was merely an accessory to van As's actions, was also prosecuted and sentenced to imprisonment with hard labour.

The case of Salmon van As

There are a number of published accounts covering the case of Assistant Field Cornet Salmon van As. On 25 September 1901, van As shot Captain Ronald Miers of the South African Constabulary (S.A.C.) near the Wolwepan, a natural pan of water south of the Suikerboschrand River, not far south of the town of Heidelberg. (Lieutenant Miers of the Somersetshire Light Infantry had transferred to the S.A.C., with the rank of captain.) Wolwepan is a small crater about 800 metres in diameter and 20 metres deep, always filled with water to a certain level, and fed from the strata beneath. It was an ideal place to keep watch on the police posts along the spruit as they and their horses were hidden from sight in the crater. The Wolwepan is four kilometres from the Suikerboschrand River, and a similar distance from de Kuilen, in the south. The confrontation between Miers and van As occurred a short distance north-east of the Wolwepan.

The S.A.C. took to the field in May 1901 and the area around Johannesburg and Pretoria, supposedly completely cleared of Boer commandos, was protected by a series of police posts. South of Heidelberg there was a line of small forts along the Suikerboschrand River, which is scarcely more than a spruit or stream in that area. Major J Fair in Heidelberg was in command of "C" Division of the S.A.C. posted to man this line. Captain A. Essex Capell was the officer in charge of the line and had his command post on the farm, De Hoek. Captain Miers was in command of a number of forts, each manned by a corporal and a few men. It seems to have been his practice to ride out to Boers whom he had seen in the distance, perhaps with a white flag, to talk with them and to persuade them to lay down their arms. He was reputed to have convinced a number of Boers to stop fighting. (Louis Slabbert's 1953 account to his daughter, Mrs Breitenbach of Ohrigstad, is quoted by H.J. Jooste in "Veldkornet Salmon van As" in *Christiaan de Wet Annale, 6*). The Boer commando, which was still in the area in September 1901, commonly made use of the Wolwepan, where they kept watch on a line of S.A.C. posts along the Suikerboschrand River.

The fatal encounter

On 25 September 1901, Corporal E.H. Woodward of the S.A.C., who was stationed in one of the forts to the north of the Wolwepan, reported that he saw "7 or 8 mounted Boers appear on the skyline to our front". Woodward said that they had a white flag and three of the party advanced on foot "slowly, making a great display with the white flag". He was reluctant to go out towards them but Corporal Tandy, from the adjacent police post, saw what was happening and went to speak with the three men. After spending "quite 10 minutes with them", according to Woodward, he cantered back and crossed the spruit at the drift (sworn statement by Archives, PMO 81, file no 37]). Tandy reported that the Boers had asked to see an officer so as "to assure them that they would not be compelled against their own countrymen" (sworn statement by Acting Corporal E J Tandy [Transvaal Archive, PMO 81 , file no 37]; Wilson, *After Pretoria*, pp798-800). Shortly thereafter, Tandy and Woodward met Captain Miers, who had his dog with him, on his grey mare. Tandy told Miers what the Boers had said. Miers reproved both corporals for having acted wrongly and foolishly. He wrote a note for Captain Capell and left his carbine and bandolier, but not his revolver, in Woodward's fort and crossed the spruit towards the Boers (sworn statement by Acting

Corporal E.H. Woodward, Transvaal Archive, PMO 81, file 37).

The British soldiers, watching from their small forts, saw one of the Boers with a white flag come forward to meet Captain Miers. After a short conversation with the man, Captain Miers went with him to the other two Boers. Shortly afterwards, the soldiers in the forts heard a faint shot and saw the Captain's mare galloping away. It later turned out that the three Boers who were involved in the incident were Salmon van As, Louis Slabbert, a young man who spoke no English, and Piet du Toit, "a thirty-year-old man (a whole lot older than I)". Slabbert had been told by van As to put his rifle down "and stop that fellow so that he does not get into our outpost". Slabbert was two hundred yards (183 metres) away from the Boer outpost when he shouted at Miers to stop. Miers ignored him and galloped up to van As. Slabbert followed on foot and was "ten yards (9 metres) behind the Englishman's horse" when a shot rang out. All Slabbert could say was, "God, Veldcornet, why did you shoot that man?" (according to war memories of Louis Slabbert as told to his daughter in 1953), but he always maintained that he had not seen what had happened. Piet du Toit would have had an even better view of the incident from his position. After the shooting, the three Boers made their way back to the farm, De Kuilen, where van As reported to a senior officer. Van As had taken Miers' revolver and binoculars and these were seen by a number of their commando colleagues. Van As always maintained that his deed was an act of war and that he had acted in self-defence.

Had van As acted in self-defence after being threatened by Miers with his revolver? We will never know. The British corporals were adamant in their sworn statements, made within a day of the shooting, that Corporal Tandy had been lured out by the Boers, who were waving a white flag, which was a recognized signal of truce. Captain Miers had stated, in his note to his senior officer that he would go out cautiously in the direction of the Boers and see if the one with the white flag would come to meet him, but he would not use a white flag. In Louis Slabbert's account to his daughter, written more than 50 years after the incident, however, he stated that Captain Miers had indeed approached them with a white flag. It is also conceivable that van As had been ordered to deal with Miers, who was a nuisance to the Boers by seeking to persuade them to lay down their arms (Louis Slabbert makes such a suggestion in the account told to his daughter, quoted by H.J. Jooste in "Veldkornet Salmon van As", *Christiaan de Wet Annale 6*, 1984).

Corporal E.H. Woodward also wrote a letter to *The Times* London, 29 November 1901) describing the incident in rather lurid detail. Whether a journalist had helped him with the letter is unknown. The letter is very well written, the facts are as stated in his sworn statements, but the language is emotive, describing how Miers' body was "stripped of everything but his shirt..." Although the Boers denied this, at that stage of the war it would have been difficult to overlook a good pair of boots and Woodward's account is not inconceivable (sworn statement by Acting Corporal E.H. Woodward, Transvaal Archives, PMO 81, file 37). Shortly after the appearance of this letter, an account appeared in H.W. Wilson's *After Pretoria*, based very much on Woodward's letter (*After Pretoria* appeared weekly and was only later bound into a large volume which appeared in May 1903). These accounts of the incident created a good deal of interest in Britain, the matter being raised by the opposition in Parliament.

The S.A.C. investigated the incident and regarded it as an act of murder. The matter was reported to Kitchener, who thereafter addressed a letter to General Louis Botha, the last sentence of which was unequivocal: "I trust your honour will see that the murderers are brought to justice." (Letter from Kitchener to Botha in the Transvaal Archives, PMO 81, file 37). Botha referred the matter to General Piet Viljoen on 28 November 1901 who replied that "he knew nothing at all of the alleged murder and no such incident has been reported by my officers" (Reply of General P.R. Viljoen to Botha's letter of 28 November in the Transvaal Archive, Preller collection, Volume 34, document 693). Commandant Alberts was also asked to investigate, but became convinced that van As was innocent of any charge and that he had acted on the orders of his superior officer and in self-defence (G.S. Preller, *Sketse en Opstelle*, p163).

Assistant Field Cornet Salmon van As was with the Heidelberg Commando at Kraal Station, south of the town, when they laid down their arms on 2 June 1902. General Louis Botha told them about the terms of peace and that they were to surrender their arms while the officers could retain theirs. He told them that van As was excluded from the amnesty provided in the peace treaty. Van As asked the general if his life was guaranteed, but Botha told him that "nothing will be done to you. There will only be an investigation" (Uys, 1981, p227).

Van As then approached Major-General Bruce Hamilton at Kraal Station and "surrendered voluntarily" according to Hamilton's letter of 7 June to Lord Kitchener (Transvaal Archives, PMO 81, file 37). By 8 June, both van As and Louis Slabbert had been arrested and were being held in the Heidelberg army camp. Piet du Toit's name was called when the other two were arrested but he was not found. Du Toit, who was thought to be a prisoner-of-war in Bermuda or India, had in fact been held in Merebank Camp in Durban. He arrived back in Heidelberg on 5 June 1902, passing the surrendered burghers at Kraal Station. He was not immediately arrested, but there is a letter in the Transvaal Archives to the effect that his trial was to take place at Pretoria. However, there is no further record that any trial ever took place.

The court martial

The court martial of van As and Slabbert took place in the Waverley Hotel between 17 and 19 June. The record of the proceedings has never been traced. The British produced, as evidence, sworn statements from three black men and six black women from the farm, De Kuilen, and, also as witnesses, Major Phillips, Corporals Woodward and Tandy, and Trooper Wallis, all of the S.A.C. The black witnesses all mentioned seeing a revolver and binoculars in the possession of van As and also boots, gaiters and other items of clothing. (The various sworn statements are in the Transvaal Archives, PMO 81, file 37). Van As was apparently fluent in English, as he had grown up in Heidelberg, which had a substantial English population at the time. He apparently cross-examined the black witnesses and destroyed their credibility as they could not have seen what had actually happened. Slabbert did not understand much of the proceedings because of his lack of English, but he clearly understood van As's cross-examination of the black witnesses, as that was conducted in Afrikaans. Nevertheless, van As was convicted of the murder of Captain Miers and sentenced to death. The court martial must have based its findings substantially on the evidence of the two corporals, and in particular on the evidence that the Boers had waved a white flag before Captain Miers rode out towards them. Louis Slabbert was sentenced to penal servitude for life, which was later varied to five years. Slabbert was released after an amnesty was given to all political prisoners and Cape and Natal Colony rebels. He eventually served twenty-one months of his sentence (See Jooste, 1984, pp63-65 for Slabbert's account of the court martial proceedings).

Execution

Salmon van As always maintained that he was innocent of murder but did not deny that he shot "one of the enemy's captains who aimed his revolver at me". Generals Piet Viljoen and Hendrik Alberts tried very hard to get in touch with General Botha in connection with the court martial, but to no avail. Viljoen visited van As in his cell the day before his execution and van As reaffirmed his innocence. Van As was executed by firing squad on Monday, 23 June 1902, standing up against the stone wall at the back of the Heidelberg jail. His body was wrapped in a blanket and buried near a thorn bush a short distance away. In October 1903, van As, General Spruyt, Commandant Kriegler and six other war casualties were reburied in the Old Heldelberg Cemetery. General Louis Botha did not attend the ceremony, although he was scheduled to be there (Uys, 1981, pp234-36; Uys, 2002, pp189-91).

In 1904, van As's father allegedly received a letter from the British Government which acknowledged that the trial had not been a fair one. Perjury had been committed (apparently by the black witnesses) and van As had not been able to call his own witnesses. A claim for compensation would be entertained but his father declined to make a claim. He blamed Louis Botha for his son's death and did not allow the mention of Botha's name in his presence (Uys, 1981, p232).

Afnkaners have always regarded Salmon van As as a martyr and a symbol of British injustice. In 1916 the well-known Afrikaans poet, c. Louis Leipoldt, composed a poem on van As which has become part of Afrikaner folklore.

Barend Celliers

The second man for whom amnesty was denied was Barend Celliers, a burgher of the Orange Free State. When General Christiaan de Wet captured the town of Dewetsdorp on 23 November 1900. a number of British soldiers were taken prisoner. Among these was Lieutenant Cecil Boyle, a member of the newly-formed Orange River Colony Police, who was Assistant District Commissioner in the town. According to Mildred Dooner (1903, 1980 reprint, p35), Boyle was A.D.C. in Lindley in the north eastern Orange Free State. Shortly thereafter, Dewetsdorp was evacuated by the Boers when de Wet headed off on what was to become an abortive attempt to invade the Cape Colony (Maurice, Vol 3, pp492-96). Boyle was taken with them. He was accused of ill-treating Boer women by making them walk instead of riding in wagons on their way to the concentration camp, as well as threatening them with a sjambok (a rawhide whip used for herding cattle and for inflicting corporal punishment). Earlier in the year, Boyle had been captured by the Boers and taken to Lesotho, where he had been warned not to take up arms again, because the next time he would be shot. (Lourens, *Te na aan ons hart*, 2002, has some details of these accusations which appeared in the *Die Volksblad* in October 1900, with the spelling, "Cilliers"). The prisoners were required to accompany the Boer expedition, but, hard-pressed by the column of Colonel Charles Knox, all the prisoners, except for Boyle, were released (Boyle was required to walk "just like the women and children" according to *Die Volksblad*, 6 October 1899).

General Philip Botha, one of de Wet's officers, an older brother of Louis Botha, was ordered to guard Boyle and took part of the commando to the Doornberg, outside Kroonstad and north of Senekal. Field Cornet Celliers was delegated to guard the captive.

On 2 January 1901 the commando was on the farm, Blijdskap, on the Liebenbergsvlei River. It was here that General Philip Botha gave Celliers his instruction that Boyle should be executed. Celliers was ordered to "take Boyle an hour's ride out of the laager and to shoot and bury him" (Rex versus Celliers, Reports of cases decided in the High Court of the Orange River Colony for 1903, p2). Celliers, accompanied by a burgher by the name of Smalberger, carried out this order. This was done on the farm "Hartebees-hoek-West", 19km south-west of Reitz. Boyle asked to write a last letter. His request was granted and, afterwards, he was shot in the back as he prayed. Boyle's documents were burned, presumably including his last letter (His family does not appear to have received it).

Celliers made no secret of his action on his return to the laager, clearly giving the impression that he had carried out the orders of a superior officer (Smallberger had apparently joined Celliers and Boyle when he was out looking for horses, according to Lourens, 2002, p226).

Celliers' commandant, Philip de Vos of the Kroonstad Commando heard what had happened and reported the matter to de Wet and President Steyn, who, on 26 January 1901, called on Celliers to account for his actions. General Philip Botha was killed in action in a small skirmish in the Doornberg on 6 March 1901 (Malan, 1990, p19; Chilvers Vol IV, 1907, p-234: and Maurice *History of the War in South Africa* Vol 4 p-93).

On 26 July 1901, Celliers was tried by a Boer court-martial at "Blijdschap", a farm near Reitz where the Orange Free State government was based for a short time. Celliers gave a statement to the court and Smalberger was called as witness. Celliers was acquitted of murder, the court martial finding that Celliers had acted under the orders of General

Philip Botha even though none of Botha's staff members were aware that such an order had been given (Lourens, 2002, p227: Neither De Vos himself, Botha's adjutant, F.J. van Reenen, or his secretary T.F. Moll).

Celliers was wounded in a later action and taken to the British military hospital in Kroonstad. Once he had recovered, he indicated under interrogation that he knew the whereabouts of the place where he had shot and buried Boyle. Together with an escort, he was sent to find the grave. The body was exhumed and reburied in the Kroonstad cemetery after being identified, apparently from his sisters' knowledge of a gold filling in one of his teeth.

Celliers was held in custody until he appeared before a jury in the High Court in Bloemfontein on 20 February 1903. The court proceedings were conducted under the Roman-Dutch law of the former Boer Republic even after the British annexation. The Presiding Judge, J. Fawkes, was a Scotsman, appointed to the Orange River Colony Bench because Scots law was much closer to Roman-Dutch than English law. At the trial, Celliers pleaded not guilty to the charge of murder. He did not deny having shot and killed Lieutenant Cecil Boyle, but his defence was that he had been acting on the orders of General Philip Botha. He was defended by J.B.M. Hertzog, who had been a judge in the Boer Republic of the Orange Free State. Hertzog at first moved that as Celliers had already been acquitted by the previous court martial, such acquittal must stand until such time as it was set aside by an appeal to a competent court. Fawkes, however, ruled that the trial must proceed as the Boer court martial had not been a competent court recognized by the Crown (Rex versus Celliers Reports of cases decided in the High Court of the Orange River Colony for 1903 pp1-7).

At the trial, Christiaan de Wet gave evidence that the former Orange Free State President, Marthinus Steyn, had suspended General Philip Botha when hearing of his action in issuing the offending order to Celliers, who was bound to obey. Smalberger, presumably the only witness to the shooting, had died before the end of the war. In the Judge's directions to the jury, he stated that "a soldier on active service was justified in obeying the order of his superior officer, provided that order was not manifestly illegal". He also directed that it was for the prisoner to prove that the order was not manifestly illegal. After deliberation, the jury acquitted Celliers and he was released.

Celliers was in many ways an outstanding burgher and fought throughout the Anglo-Boer war with the Kroonstad Commando. He was wounded five times, and his last wounding unfortunately brought him into the hospital at Hoopstad, where he was captured by the British. After Celliers' acquittal, he lived on his farm "Stinkhoutboom" near Vredefort. He was a follower of de Wet and was involved in the rebellion of 1914. General C.F. Beyers and a number of men, including Celliers, were trapped by Union forces against the Vaal River and Beyers was drowned attempting to cross. In 1920 Celliers was elected to the Provincial Council of the Orange Free State and in 1935 he became a senator in the Union parliament. He died in 1947 and is buried on his farm (Malan, 1990, p68).

Josef Muller

Josef Muller, a burgher from the Vrede district, was the third Boer who was required to stand trial for murder after the cessation of hostilities. Five Rademan brothers, from the farm Raaikloof in the Harrismith district, were unwilling from the very outset to defend their fatherland and join the war on the Boer side. One of them, Marthinus, crossed the border into Natal and lived in Newcastle for the duration of the war. The other brothers hid in the mountains so as to avoid commando service. One brother, Johannes Jacobus, was captured by the Boers and held for a while in the jail at Harrismith. He was then sent over the border into Natal, apparently to prevent him giving any assistance to the British.

John Frederick Rademan was the subject of a story in the *Natal Mercury*, 18 February 1901. The story ran under the headline "The Murder of John Rademan" and told how Rademan had refused to join the burghers on commando on the grounds that he was unwilling to break the oath of neutrality that he had signed. President Steyn had refused to acknowledge the oath and Rademan's attitude enraged his fellow countrymen. The newspaper reported, wrongly, that he had been shot at his farm, Raaikloof, but did not name his adversaries.

It appears that John Rademan had in fact been called up on commando but had deserted and tried to hide at his mother's farm near Memel. In December 1900 a burgher, Josef Muller, was ordered by Field Cornet Charles Meintjies to bring him back, dead or alive. When the burghers went to get him, Rademan refused to leave with them. Allegedly, Rademan went for his rifle and Muller shot him dead. If this was the case then certainly Muller acted in self-defence (For more information on Josef Muller see Blake, 2010, pp215-17).

Another brother, Cornelius Johannes Rademan, claimed after the war that he had never been on commando and escaped military service by claiming that he was medically unfit. After the shooting of his brother John in December 1900 he went over the border into Natal, acted as a guide for a British column and was even paid the considerable sum of £400 for his services.

There is no record of Josef Muller having been tried for the murder of John Rademan.

References

1. Blake, Albert, *Boereverraaier* Tafelberg, Cape Town 2010.
2. Chilvers, Hedley (ed), *The Times History of the War in South Africa*, Vol V Sampson Low, Marston and Co Ltd, London 1907.
3. De Villiers, J.C. (Kay), *Healers, Helpers and Hospitals* Protea Book House, Pretoria 2008.
4. Dooner, Mildred G., *The Last Post* J.B. Hayward & Son, Polstead, Suffolk, 1980 (reprint of edition of 1903).
5. Jooste, H J, "Veldkornet Salmon van As" in *Christiaan de Wet Annale 6* Die Suid-Afrikaanse Akademie vir Wetenskap en Kuns in samewerking met die Oorlogsmuseum, Bloemfontein, Oktober 1984.

6. Kestell, The Rev J.D., & van Velden, D.E., *The Peace Negotiations* Richard Clay & Sons, Ltd, London 1912.
7. Lourens, J. and J.A.J., *Te na aan ons hart: Aspekte van die Anglo-Boereoorlog in die Reitz omgewing* Privately published 2002.
8. Malan, Jacques, *Die Boere-Offisiere van die Tweede Vryheidsoorlog, 1899-1902* J.P. van der Walt, Pretoria 1990.
9. Maurice, Major-General Sir Frederick, *History of the War in South Africa*, Volumes 3&4 Hurst & Blackett Limited, London 1908 & 1910 respectively.
10. Scholtz, David, "Lieutenant Cecil D. Boyle: Summary of the circumstances of the shooting of Lieutenant Cecil D Boyle by Commandant Barend Celliers and the latter's subsequent trial in Bloemfontein" (unpublished document).
11. Uys, Ian, *Heidelbergers of the Boer War* Ian Uys, Heidelberg 1981.
12. Uys, Ian, *Fight to the Bitter End* Fortress Financial Group [Pty] Ltd, Knysna 2002.
13. Wilson, H W, *After Pretoria II* London 1903.
14. Reports of cases decided in the High Court of the Orange River Colony for 1903.

Wolwepan

The last that was seen of Captain Miers.

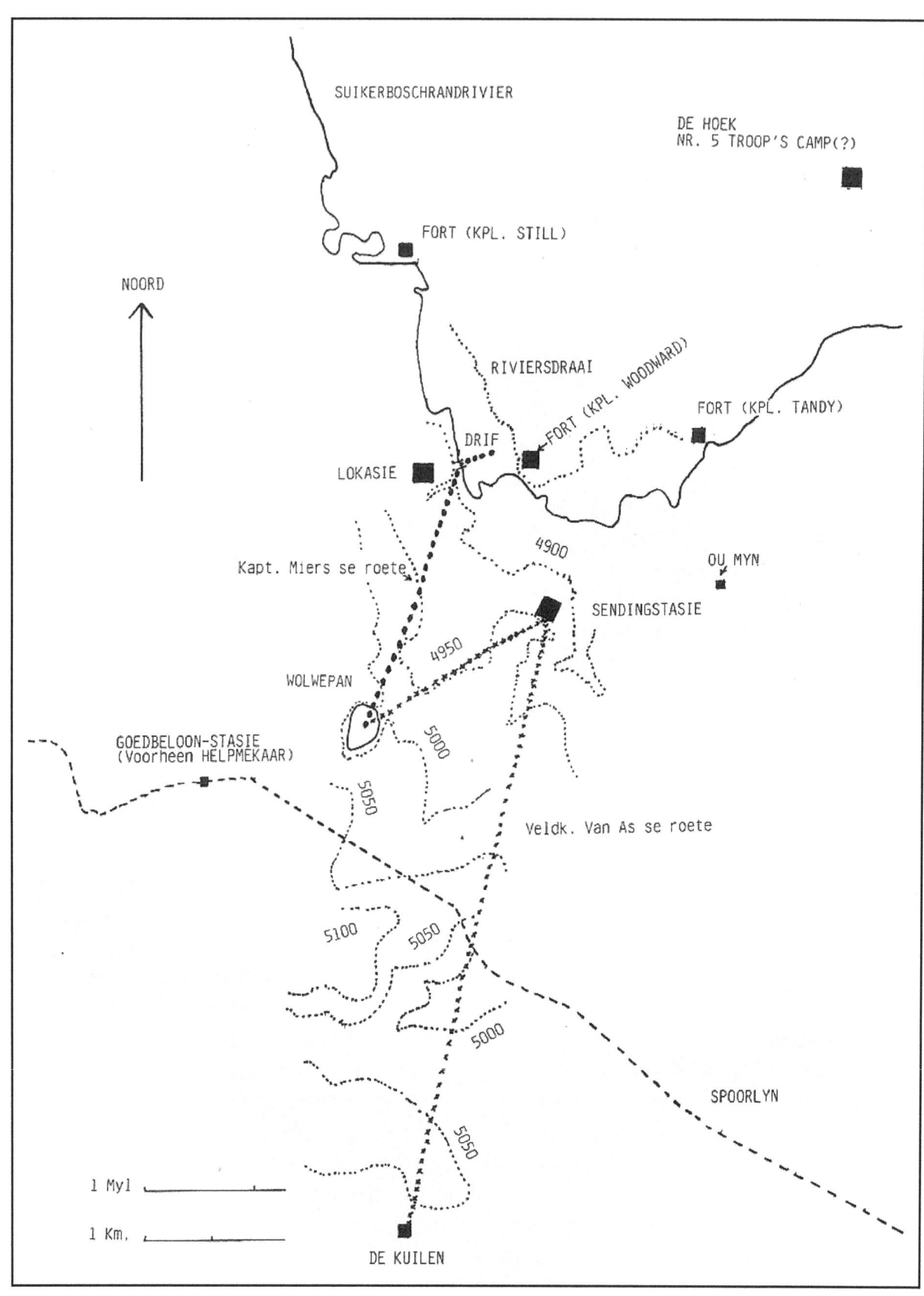

Map from H.J. Jooste *Veldcornet Salmon van As* from *De Wet Annale 6*.

Heidelberg commando at Kraal Station 5 June 1902: Salmon van As is seated at the left; Commandant Alberts in the centre; General Piet Viljoen seated second right.
Below: Assistant Field Cornet Salmon van As; Lieutenant Ronald Miers.

Old Gaol, Heidelberg: Scene of van As's execution.

"Salmon van As" – poem by C. Louis Leipoldt

Daar's 'n droevige volksvergadering
Waar Vereeniging kijk oor die veld,
En dapperste vaderlandsliefde
Moet swig onder snode geweld,
En lewe lijk duurder als doodgaan
Vir hom wat op eer is gesteld.
Die oorlog is eindelik geëindig
Net soos hij begin was: met moed;
Die smart en die lang reeks verliese
Moet stadig deur vlijt word vergoed,
En Vereenigings-vrede bekragtig
Deur Salmon van As met sij bloed.

There's a sorrowful national assembly,
Where Vereeniging looms in the field,
And the bravest patriotism
To wicked power must yield,
And life seems harder than dying
To those who keep honour for their shield.
The war has finally ended,
Just as it began: with hope.
The sorrow and series of losses
Must slowly by toil be coped,
And for sealing the peace of Vereeniging
Van As's blood is the dope.

(Translated from Afrikaans by
Professor Dr C. de Jong)

Above: General Philip Botha; General J.B.M. Hertzog.

Below: Commandant Barend Celliers; Field Cornet Charles Meintjies.

Val in the Anglo-Boer War

The Anglo-Boer War was an eventful time for the small community

There was a great deal of activity around the station of Val during the Anglo-Boer war with the Heidelberg and Standerton commandos active in the area. As it was a station on the main line from Johannesburg to Natal, a vital supply line for the British army in Johannesburg, Val was heavily guarded by both the South African Constabulary and the British army. Armoured trains, which could rush reinforcements to any part of the line, operated out of Standerton and Heidelberg. Notwithstanding these security measures, Boer commandos derailed more than 60 trains in 1901 and 1902 on the stretch of railway line between Volksrust and Johannesburg.

There were numerous small actions to the north and south of the village and its station. After the British forces reached Val on their way to Johannesburg and Pretoria, the railway line needed frequent repairs and maintenance to keep traffic flowing. Continual vigilance was exercised to guard against the Boers and their forays with dynamite and gunpowder. This article covers events concerning trooper Angus Jenkins, the "*Whisky Train*" and Surgeon-Captain Arthur Martin-Leake VC. There are monuments to them and others around Val. There is also a memorial to the Boer Kommandant, Gert Marthinus Claassen, on the farm Syferfontein, where Martin-Leake had been based immediately before the engagement with the Boers in which he won his first Victoria Cross. Gert Claassen was the Commandant of one of the Standerton Commandos during the First World War and took part in the invasion of German South West Africa under General Louis Botha. France awarded him the Croix de Guerre for his services.

Hostilities commenced in the Anglo-Boer war when General Piet Joubert's Boer forces crossed into the Colony of Natal on the expiry of their ultimatum on 11 October 1899. It took some time before the war reached the small village of Val, barely more than a halt on the main railway line from Pretoria to Durban. For some months all that the people of the village and its surrounding farms would have seen was the traffic on the line. The actual fighting was a fair distance away with Ladysmith besieged by the Boers and the British attacks on the Boer lines along the Tugela River in attempts to relieve the town which were finally successful on 28 March 1900.

After the relief of Ladysmith, British General Redvers Buller and his Natal Field Force army moved forward early in May, 1900. They entered the Transvaal after battles at Botha's Pass on 6 and 7 June and Allemansnek on 11th. The advance guard entered Volksrust on the 12th, by the 22nd Standerton was occupied. At this time Lord Roberts had occupied Johannesburg and Pretoria and driven Louis Botha's forces away to the east after dislodging them from Diamond Hill on 11 and 12 June.

What was needed now was for the railway line between Heidelberg and Standerton to be secured and then heavily guarded. This became an important additional line of supply between Durban and Johannesburg and a vital lifeline for Roberts's army. Buller gave orders to Lieutenant General Sir Francis Clery's 2nd Division to link up with Major-General Ian Hamilton's force occupying Heidelberg.

Lord Strathcona's Horse, a Canadian unit, had only recently joined the Natal Field Force, an élite regiment composed of men from the north western provinces of Canada: Saskatchewan, Manitoba, Alberta and British Columbia. On 31 December 1899 the wealthy Canadian High Commissioner to the UK, Lord Strathcona, offered to raise a military unit of mounted riflemen at his own expense. He was clearly concerned about the implications of "Black Week", when the British army suffered defeats at the hands of the irregular forces of the Boers at Stormberg, Magersfontein and Colenso on 10, 11 and 15 December 1899. He cabled his proposal to the Canadian Prime Minister, Wilfred Laurier, who readily agreed, but subject to the approval of the British War Office and the Canadian Militia Department. This was readily given and in March 1900 this homogeneous corps, being composed entirely of men from one region, left Canada on its way to South Africa.

Strathcona was a remarkable man, nearing 80 years of age in 1900, who had investments in the Hudson Bay Company as well as railroads, insurance and banking. He at first did not want his name to be associated with the project. However, it was announced in the Canadian press shortly after his "munificent offer" was accepted by the British War Office and the Canadian Militia Department. Strathcona wanted four hundred (later raised to five hundred) mounted men, all from the Canadian North-West, "proficient and experienced rough riders and rangers, unmarried, expert marksmen and at home in the saddle." He also insisted that all officer appointments must be approved by him personally.

Strathcona certainly had no difficulty with the appointment of Colonel Sam B. Steele to command Lord Strathcona's Horse. Steele was 50 years of age in 1899 and had been a soldier or policemen from the age of 16. He was "an energetic, shrewd, tough, but diplomatic manager of men...with no regard for the stupidities of barrack square drill." Many of the other officers were police inspectors from the North-West Mounted Police given the rank of Major or Captain. Horses were all from the Canadian North-West but many were lost on the voyage to Cape Town, so many in fact that someone unkindly christened the regiment Strathcona's Foot. With remounts, they were sent to Natal to join General Redvers Buller's Natal Field Force. They made a serious impression on Frank Crozier, a Trooper in the colonial regiment Thorneycroft's Mounted Infantry, who described them as "strange men in Stetson hats, big fellows all with brown boots and slightly different uniforms..."

Strathcona's Horse joined the 3rd Mounted Brigade under Brigadier General the Earl of Dundonald during June. In effect, Strathcona's Horse replaced the Natal Volunteers whose government did not permit them to operate outside the borders of the Colony. Colonel Steele insisted that his men were scouts, "doing any important work that experienced horsemen and good shots can do". He insisted that they be engaged in scouting, outpost and patrol work and not assigned to garrison duty.

Dundonald wrote that "the work of cavalry in this difficult country was arduous in the extreme; without the excitement of a general action there were daily losses." He had spoken to his men before they entered the Transvaal: "You have seen the devastation by the Boers in Natal. Don't go in for revenge. Respect the property of the Boers and pay for everything that you want."

On 1 July Strathcona's Horse furnished a detachment, "A" and "B" Squadrons, to scout and do reconnaissance on the right flank of the 2nd Division. Clery had camped the previous night at Val on the main line between Johannesburg and Durban, about 20kms east of Greylingstad, and reached Greylingstad that day. The regimental diary states that the weather was fine and that they marched at 7:30 a.m., "crossing the spruit at Smith's Store". This "spruit" must have been the Waterval River, which flows to the east of Val. "The column had stopped for a rest and a hasty lunch at noon when it was interrupted by two scouts coming in at the gallop." Lieutenants Tobin and Kirkpatrick led their men towards a farmhouse that was flying a white flag, signifying that the farm was supposedly safe to approach. The men had been warned to be cautious about approaching the white flag. Boer patrols, perhaps unbeknown to the farm owners, made use of kraals and outbuildings for concealment.

A Boer force was concealed in an orchard and waiting for the Canadians to get close. One of Kirkpatrick's men, Trooper Angus Jenkins, was killed in a volley of fire and Sergeant Herbert Nichol's horse was shot and killed. Dundonald described the incident as murder, "mostly by strangers to the locality and not by the farmer." Jenkins had been a "cowpuncher" according to his attestation papers, before joining Lord Strathcona's Horse and was just 20 years of age.

The Canadians retired a short distance under cover and the reserve moved up in support. In the meantime "A" battery Royal Horse Artillery shelled the position and the enemy retired. They had run into a patrol of General Ben Viljoen's force that was shadowing the British advance along the railway to Greylingstad. The skirmish took place on the farm Witnek but it is not possible to pinpoint exactly where it happened. Jenkins was buried in the orchard of the farm and the funeral was attended by Lord Dundonald and Colonel Steele. Jenkins was the first casualty of Strathcona's Horse and was killed on an important public holiday in Canada, Dominion Day. His body was recovered some years later and he is probably now buried with a number of other Canadians in the Garden of Remembrance in Standerton cemetery. There is also a legend that his body was moved after the war by local farmers to their family cemetery on the farm Paardefontein. There is a memorial over this grave. Three more men of Strathcona's were killed in action during July in small skirmishes and clashes north of the railway line.

The war had now arrived at Val. Once Johannesburg, Pretoria and Lydenburg had been captured by Lord Roberts's army, the Natal railway line became one of the lifelines for supplies of food and munitions for the British army. The stretch of line between Standerton and Heidelberg was particularly vulnerable to attack. The Heidelbergers of Commandant Fanie Buys were especially adept at blowing up trains, culverts and even bridges. The British eventually protected their railways with blockhouses sited at intervals of one thousand yards but in 1900 these little forts had yet to be built. More than thirty trains were blown up and derailed on this stretch of line before these defensive measures could be put in place.

In December 1900, Commandant Buys selected a likely place where a successful attack could be made on a passing train. The elevated line passed over a small stone culvert a short distance up the line from Val station. Undulations in the ground provided hiding places for the two men who must lay and detonate the mine. Two brothers were given that task and they spent several hours one night burying a bag of black powder between the lines. They used a magneto generator to explode the charge but only had two hundred yards of wire so they had to hide themselves nearer than this to the train – and the explosion!

The brothers were Jack and Gert van den Heever and Jack later wrote an entertaining account of their night's work in a little book published in the 1940s called *Op Kommando onder Kommandant Fanie Buys*. The quality of the writing is such that their relative, C.M. van den Heever, must surely have lent a hand. The mine exploded under the goods train and several trucks turned over and rolled down the embankment. Buys's Heidelbergers galloped up to find a cargo of good cheer for the Christmas and New Year celebrations in Johannesburg and Pretoria spread liberally along the railway line. The war was forgotten and the party that ensued involved the Tommys on the train as well as Buys's men. Jack and Gert seem to have been the instigators. Indeed Jack, rather inebriated after perhaps an excess of sampling the many wares, extracted permission from one of the older commando members to marry one of his daughters – which he duly did once the war was over. A memorial has been erected at the site of the incident.

A meeting between General Louis Botha and the British commander-in-chief general, Lord Kitchener, had taken place in Middelburg on 28 February 1901. Mrs Botha, living in Pretoria, had been given a letter to deliver to her husband, wherein it was proposed that Botha and Kitchener should meet to see if common ground could be found to arrange terms of peace. Anything and everything was open to discussion "except that the question of independence of the two republics was not to be discussed in any way". The question of independence, however, was certainly going to be Botha's first point of departure during the meeting, but nevertheless details of a process leading to a cessation of hostilities were discussed in a reasonable and even friendly spirit. Botha clearly realised that, at some time or another, the war could only be ended by negotiation. A letter was sent to the British High Commissioner, Lord Milner, and then to the British Government, who returned it for Kitchener to send a final version to Botha, who declined to negotiate further.

A letter was sent to the Government Secretary of the Orange Free State after a meeting of the Transvaal government and their generals on 10 May 1901. This letter suggested an approach to Kitchener for permission to send ambassadors to Europe to place before President Kruger "the condition of our country". Furthermore, it was proposed that an armistice be requested so as to decide "what we must do". President Steyn was very disappointed with the sentiments expressed in this letter and insisted that a joint meeting of the two Republican governments be organised somewhere on the Transvaal Highveld at an agreed venue as soon as possible.

Following representations from Louis Botha and Acting Transvaal President Schalk Burger, Kitchener permitted the Boers to send a telegram to President Kruger in Holland. This was done via the Netherlands Consul and using their cipher. Kruger's reply was to the effect that the Boers should fight on even though there was little chance of any intervention by a European power. He said that there were some signs of public opinion in Britain becoming opposed to the war. As he was now remote from the war, he felt that any decisions should be taken jointly by the two Republican governments. Kruger's telegram was an important document tabled at the meeting in the Branddrift farmhouse.

On 20 June 1901, a Boer *krygsraad* took place which had been preceded and indeed precipitated by the earlier meeting at Middelburg on 28 February 2001. This brought about some vital decisions on Boer plans for the future. At first the meeting was convened in a secluded place somewhere along the Waterval River, in an area practically denuded of human and animal population as a result of the British "scorched earth" policy. The meeting was then moved to the nearby Branddrift farmhouse alongside the drift of the same name over the Waterval River. This farmhouse was close to Kromdraai where General Ben Viljoen camped with his commando on several occasions. Branddrift was the most secure place which the Boers could find in an area crisscrossed by British columns. They kept well away from both railway lines – the main Johannesburg-Natal line and the ZASM line from Pretoria to Delagoa Bay (now Maputo). Blockhouses, only one thousand yards (914m) apart and connected by barbed wire, now protected the lines. Armoured trains operated on each of these lines and British reinforcements could be rushed to any point where they might be needed. Boer scouts kept the area around Branddrift under constant surveillance, for security was absolutely vital. (Local oral tradition has it that the Boers even had a sentry on the roof of the farmhouse.)

The Branddrift farmhouse was a sufficient distance north of Val so that the Boer leaders were not detected by British patrols and columns. The Transvaalers made their way from the hills around Amsterdam and, with some difficulty, evaded pursuing British columns. General Ben Viljoen provided the escort and the scouts who brought them safely to the farmhouse at Branddrift. At the meeting were Acting Transvaal President Schalk Burger and Orange Free State President Marthinus Steyn, Transvaal State Secretary Francis Reitz, Commandant-General Louis Botha and Chief Commandant Christiaan de Wet, Generals Hertzog, Viljoen, Spruyt, De la Rey, Smuts, Muller, Lucas Meyer and a number of other commandants and officers. Should the British have managed to locate this concentration of the entire senior leadership of the two republics, the capture of even a few of them would have been disastrous for the Boer war effort. The principal reason for the meeting was for the Boers to decide whether or not to continue the war, but a number of other matters needed to be discussed as well, and important decisions needed to be made. Steyn was in no doubt about his determination to fight on to the bitter end, but recent Boer successes made this matter almost a foregone conclusion for the Boer leadership. Boer successes at Vlakfontein in the western Transvaal (now North West Province) on 29 May and Wilmansrust on 12 June had given them encouragement enough. Thus it was resolved "that no peace shall be made, and no peace proposals entertained that do not ensure our independence and our existence as a nation". After this there were no more joint meetings of the two Republican governments until the April 1902 consultations in Klerksdorp when it was agreed to approach the British with a joint proposal for negotiations about peace.

On 8 February 1902 another interesting event took place in the vicinity of Val. At the time, the Anglo-Boer war was winding down and both sides were considering making overtures about bringing hostilities to an end.

The Victoria Cross is Britain's premier award for gallantry. It was instituted by Royal Warrant on 29 January 1856 for award to both officers and non-commissioned ranks of the Royal Navy and the Army who, in the presence of the enemy "shall have performed some signal act of valour...". Arthur Martin-Leake twice performed such signal acts, in the Anglo-Boer War in 1902 and again in the Great War in 1914. He was the first man to be twice honoured with the award of the Victoria Cross for each of his exploits. Only two others have since managed to emulate Martin-Leake's feat, Captain Noel Chavasse in 1915 and 1916 and Captain Charles Upham in 1941 and 1942.

Arthur Martin-Leake was born in 1874 to a family in comfortable circumstances. He entered the University College Hospital in London in 1893 and qualified as a doctor in February 1899. As a student, Martin-Leake worked under Victor Horsley, the foremost neuro-surgeon of his age, assisting or witnessing numbers of his operations on the brain and spinal cord. He qualified as a doctor in February 1899 and obtained membership of the Royal College of Surgeons. Martin-Leake was House Surgeon at the West Hertfordshire Infirmary when war was declared in South Africa. There was a widespread feeling that the war would be over by Christmas and Arthur was concerned that he might miss this great adventure. Leave from his duties was readily given by the hospital authorities who clearly shared his patriotic spirit.

A new force, the Imperial Yeomanry, was to be raised and Martin-Leake joined the 42nd (Hertfordshire) Company. Disgruntled with his pay and conditions, lack of facilities for study, prospects for advancement and reluctant to join the Royal Army Medical Corps, Martin-Leake managed to join the South African Constabulary in May 1901. In October 1901 he was transferred to Syferfontein, a short distance north of Val, as medical officer of "C" Division of the S.A.C. On Syferfontein (or Cyferfontein), there was a large farmhouse which had been taken over by the S.A.C. as a fortified post. The stone-built house, which still stands, was close to the Waterval River, which meant a reliable supply of fresh water.

The South African Constabulary had been formed under the leadership and command of Major General Robert S.S. Baden-Powell. He had become famous after his celebrated defence of Mafeking. Besieged by the Boer forces of the Zuid Afrikaansche Republiek, he held the town for 215 days until relieved in May 1900. Promoted to Major General, he was given the responsibility of recruiting and training the South African Constabulary, a para-military police force for the maintenance of law and order in the Transvaal and Orange Free State, by then annexed as British territory.

The "C" Division of the S.A.C. manned a line of police posts which stretched between the two main railway lines, the line from Johannesburg to Natal and the Pretoria-Delagoa Bay line. Originally the line of Constabulary posts connected the railway lines from Eerstefabrieken, east of Pretoria, to Heidelberg. In September 1901 the line was moved further east to between Wilge River Station and Greylingstad. In November the line was moved still further east from Brugspruit on the Delagoa line to Waterval on the Natal railway, with an extension to Villiersdorp (today Villiers). The area east and west of the line around Johannesburg and Pretoria was the so-called "protected area" and was supposedly clear of Boers.

Intelligence reports, probably from local African inhabitants, persistently indicated that a Boer force had encroached into the protected area. Although these were mostly discredited, an order from the Commander-in-Chief, General Lord Kitchener, for the line of posts to move further forward, caused Major Fair to order a reconnaissance preparatory to making such a move. The party consisted of 150 men drawn from three troops of "C" Division under the command of Captain Algernon Essex Capell. They assembled at Syferfontein. As Medical Officer, Martin-Leake accompanied the patrol which was seeking to locate the Boer laager which had encroached into the protected area.

The patrol set off from Syferfontein at 4 a.m. on 8 February 1902 at which time it would be at least another forty-five minutes before it would even start to get light. They proceeded north east towards the neighbouring farm Vlakfontein and on towards Van Tondershoek. The intelligence was specific that it was on this farm that they might find the Boer laager. The intelligence proved to be accurate. The Boers were hidden in a deep hollow fed by a stream which, even today, has running water summer and winter. A short distance from the hollow was the original Van Tondershoek farmhouse.

These Boers were the men of General Piet Viljoen. After suffering severe losses from British raids at Trichaardsfontein and Witkrans, he had returned to his base at Vaalkop, north of Bethal. Thus his strategy was to move west into the protected area. With 200 men, Commandant Joachim Prinsloo and Field Cornet J.C. Duvenhage made the first incursion into the protected area to be followed on 24 January by another 400 men of the Pretoria, Germiston and Heidelberg commandos. This force, now consisting of perhaps 600 rifles, was what was uncovered by Captain Capell's patrol.

Capell's men seem to have rather injudiciously opened fire on the laager but his 150 men were greatly outnumbered. How many Boers were in the laager is a matter of some conjecture. Some accounts say 800, almost certainly an exaggeration – but 600 is credible. If Capell's patrol was able to get as close as 400 yards without detection it is likely that the Boers lay hidden until the last possible moment.

When it became obvious that their lair had been detected, they returned fire and attempted to outflank the policemen on both sides.

Now came an orderly retirement back to base at Syferfontein. There were experienced fighters on each side and the running fight took them back over Vlakfontein. The S.A.C. left and right flank guards were fiercely attacked by the Boers and found themselves unable to join the rest of Captain Capell's men who got away safely. Capell managed to get most of the left flank away but eight men, a Sergeant and an Officer and the Medical Officer, Captain Martin-Leake, were unable to find a way to escape. They were engaging some Boers at a distance of 1,600 yards and seemed to be secure until a group of Boers crept up a small donga and opened fire from a flank. All eight men were quickly killed or wounded. Martin-Leake moved up and down the firing line attending to the wounded. All the men of this small section of the force were either killed or wounded, including Martin-Leake.

Martin-Leake attended to a number of the men, dressing their wounds and controlling bleeding, all that could be done while under fire. Sergeant Waller was hit in the leg and severely wounded. Martin-Leake attended to him, apparently oblivious of the heavy close-range fire. When Lieutenant Abraham suffered a mortal injury, Martin-Leake ran over to him in an attempt to make him more comfortable and ease his pain. It was here that the doctor was shot three times, being wounded in the right hand and left thigh.

The Boers overran the little group but were not inclined to take prisoners. They left them where they lay, expressing regret that they had shot the doctor, and disappeared back the way they had come. The wounded and dead lay where they had fallen for some hours. Help arrived, probably after dark, bringing stretchers, blankets, bandages and water. Men when severely wounded quickly develop a raging thirst and lying for hours in the hot sun must have been agonising. There was at first a limited amount of water but Martin-Leake refused to take his share until all the others had been served.

After the incident at Vlakfontein, Martin-Leake was taken to hospital in Heidelberg where his thigh wound healed easily, as did his hand, except that the ulnar nerve had been severed, causing the hand to be paralysed. This was a disabling wound for a man wishing to become a surgeon but an operation in England in June by Sir Victor Horsley joined the nerve ends and seems to have been partially successful, leaving Martin-Leake with a permanent loss of flexibility.

For his bravery under heavy fire, Martin-Leake was awarded his first Victoria Cross. The Victoria Cross was conferred on him by King Edward VII at Windsor Castle on 2 June 1902, the very first post-war ceremony for the presentation of awards and medals.

A further interesting event took place at Val in the closing stages of the Anglo-Boer war. Boer leaders from the Zuid-Afrikaansche Republiek (the Transvaal) and the Orange Free State were to meet in Klerksdorp to decide whether to continue with the war or to negotiate peace terms with the British Government. The Boer governments' intentions needed to be clarified. The usual democratic fashion of the Boers required a *krygsraad* to ratify any move to initiate talks with the British. This time, however, there could be no question that discussions were about to begin in Klerksdorp.

There is a famous picture of the Boer leaders about to take a train from Val Station to Klerksdorp. This was on 6 April 1902 and on that day Val was famous as the picture went around the world. Commandant-General Louis Botha had arrived at the station in a Cape cart the previous day, accompanied by an escort of commandos. Botha and a number of Boer officers, now under safe conduct from the British, met in a room of the Val Hotel, which still stands on the northern side of the station. Hardliners among his officers were against any kind of negotiation with the British and the Boer governments' intentions needed to be clarified. In that meeting with the Boer officers in a room in the Val Hotel on 6 April 1902, Botha surely had some hard talking to do.

It had been six months since the Waterval *kreigsraad* before there was this further development which was to lead eventually to the Peace of Vereeniging. After three days of discussions in Klerksdorp, it was agreed that the Boer leaders should meet with Kitchener in Pretoria so as to put forward their proposals. On 12 April the Boer leaders presented their views, but the two sides were still far apart. Therefore it was resolved that the Boers would select thirty representatives from each of the two republics to meet in Vereeniging. These delegates were to decide among themselves what would constitute a new set of proposals to present to the British Government representatives, Sir Alfred Milner and General Lord Kitchener. Nearing the end of May, with the sixty Boer delegates still not having come to some definite conclusion, a draft peace treaty was telegraphed to the British Government, which responded on 28 May with their counter proposal. A deadline of midnight on 31 May was imposed. The British deadline of midnight on 31 May was met with a few minutes to spare. If a peace agreement was not signed by that time then hostilities would recommence. Ten Boer leaders met at Melrose House in Pretoria and put their signatures to the Peace of Vereeniging. The hard talking at Val Hotel, when General Louis Botha was harangued by his officers, was surely part of the lengthy process.

Some parts of the Val Hotel date back to the 1890s – it certainly was the finest hotel in the area at the time of the Anglo-Boer war (as it still is!) Val has looked after its heritage. All the memorials in the area bear witness to some extraordinary happenings during the tragic three years of war in what became South Africa.

Trooper Angus Jenkins: As a policeman in the North West Territories Mounted Police and shortly before joining Lord Strathcona's Horse. And what a wonderful horse!

Vlakfontein – 8 February 1902: Surgeon-Captain Arthur Martin-Leake attends to the wounded and earns the award of the Victoria Cross. He gained a bar to his medal when was rewarded with another in 1914 during the Great War.

The site of the derailment of the whisky train in December 1900.

General Louis Botha arrives at Val, 5 April 1902.

Generals Louis and Chris Botha at Val Station on 6 April 1902. Chris facing to the left with a badge in his slouch hat and Louis in front of him, nearer to the carriage and also facing to the left.

The memorials to Trooper Angus Jenkins and Surgeon-Captain Arthur Martin-Leake.

INDEX

Airey, 30, 32, 33
Albert Blake, 102, 103, 105
Australian, 8, 26, 29-33, 39, 51, 67-70, 76-78, 81, 83, 92, 114-115, 135
Baden-Powell, 11, 26, 29, 31-34, 39, 41, 152, 164, 202
Beatson, 77, 79, 80, 82-84
Bell, 77-78, 83, 126, 147
Benson, 14, 105, 122, 123, 124-126, 132
Bethune's Mounted Infantry, 11-12, 14
Bindon Blood, 77, 79, 82-83, 122
Botha, 8-9, 11-12, 19, 29, 31-32, 34-35, 38, 40, 49, 51, 66, 91-94, 96, 100, 105, 122-125, 132-136, 141-142, 166, 173-174, 190-194, 199-202, 204, 206
Bouwer, 98, 100-103, 107-109
Brakpan, 77-78, 83
Branddrift, 91-93, 105, 202
Brandwater Basin, 8, 38, 49
Buller, 11-12, 18-19, 49, 200
Campbell, 35, 77-78, 126
Campbell-Bannerman, 9
Carrington, 31
Cecil, 29, 193-194
Chamberlain, 19, 30, 168
Clery, 18-20, 200-201
Colenso, 7, 19, 30, 200
De Klipdrift, 174, 176-177
de la Rey, 9, 29, 32, 34, 40, 49-51, 66-67, 76, 91-93, 122, 135, 165, 167, 173-175, 177, 188, 190-191, 202
de Lisle, 51-53, 125, 166
de Wet, 8-9, 38-39-41, 44-46, 49-52, 58, 65-66, 76-77, 82, 91-94, 96, 135, 143, 145, 153, 165-168, 172-173-175, 191-194, 196, 202
Diamond Hill, 18, 29, 31, 38-39, 49, 66, 142, 200
Drotsky, 82-83
du Moulin, 115-116, 142-147
Dundonald, 11-12, 20, 200-201
Emily Back, 33-34, 37
Forrest, 35, 78-79
French, 11, 30, 38, 105, 142
Haig, 107-109
Hamilton, 13-14, 39-41, 46, 94, 125, 133, 135, 167, 175, 192
Hertzog, 50, 91, 143-144, 165, 191, 194, 199, 202
Imperial Light Horse, 11-12, 26-27, 30, 67-68, 70, 74, 77, 115, 118, 123, 135-136, 152, 167, 175-176
Imperial Yeomanry, 40, 51, 115, 133-134, 202
Jenkins, 18-22, 24, 200-201, 204, 206
Joubert, 8, 11, 25

Kimberley, 7, 11, 18-19, 25, 28, 30-31, 38, 122, 143, 173
Kimberley Mounted Corps, 26-27, 30
Kitchener, 7-9, 39, 66, 76-77, 83, 91-92, 94, 115, 122-123, 125, 143, 153-154, 165, 174-175, 190-192, 201-204
Kritzinger, 114-115, 117, 142
Kroonstad, 38, 49, 52, 166, 175, 190, 193-194
Kruger, 7, 19, 39-40, 49, 51, 66, 76, 82, 92, 100-101, 123, 201-202
Krugersdorp, 31, 39-40, 50, 66-67, 142, 152
Ladysmith, 7, 11-12, 20, 25-27, 38, 67, 77, 133, 200
Lansdowne, 7, 190
Laurier, 19, 200
Le Gallais, 2, 50-53, 56, 62-63, 176
Lilley, 2, 116-117, 135-136
Lloyd, 68, 70, 91, 127
Lord Strathcona's Horse, 18-21, 24, 200-201, 204
Mafeking, 7, 11, 18, 25-31, 38-39, 83, 114, 152, 175, 203
Magersfontein, 7, 19, 30, 122, 200
Mahon, 25-26, 30, 39-41
Martin-Leake, 152-155, 158-159, 162-163, 200, 202-203, 205-206
McKnight, 79-83
Methuen, 32, 39-40, 44, 46, 122, 143, 173-174, 177
Middelburg, 9, 77-79, 82-84, 91-92, 94, 123-124, 165, 190, 201-202
Milner, 7, 9, 19, 91-92, 114, 116, 118, 152, 190, 201, 204
Muller, 67-69, 78, 80-82, 84, 91, 190-191, 194, 202
Natal Carbineers, 12, 18
New Zealand, 7-8, 26, 30, 39, 41, 67, 69-70, 77, 115, 117-118, 133, 142, 165-167
Newcastle, 12, 18, 194
Nieuwoudt, 142-145
Opperman, 99, 124, 133-134, 141
Otter, 79, 82, 115
Paget, 66-69
Plumer, 26-27, 29-31, 67, 69, 71, 114-117, 133, 135, 141-142
Pooley, 115-118, 121, 135
Pulteney, 77, 133
Queensland 30-33, 67-70, 74, 77, 115, 117-118, 133-136
Rawlinson, 114, 122-123, 133, 175
Reitz, 10, 49, 91-92, 100, 105, 107-109, 165, 193, 202
Richardson, 18, 21, 24, 128

Roberts, 7, 11, 14, 25, 27, 29, 31, 38-40, 49-50, 66-67, 70, 76, 81, 98, 122, 152, 167-168, 200
Roodewal, 40, 175-176, 178, 182, 186
Royston, 77
Rustenburg, 28-29, 31-34, 39-40, 152, 175
Salisbury, 7, 19, 26
Scheepers, 40, 98, 100
Scheeper's Nek, 11-14, 16-17
Schikkerling, 80-81, 84
Schimmelhoek, 123-125, 133, 137
Scottish, 77, 114, 123-124, 126-128
Smith-Dorrien, 190
Smuts, 34, 38, 91, 93, 98, 105, 107-109, 114-115, 117, 122, 142, 165, 191, 202
Stebbins, 83
Steele, 18-21, 200-201
Steyn, 7-8, 39-40, 49-52, 65-66, 76, 82, 91-92, 96, 165-167, 172-173, 175, 190, 193-194, 202
Stormberg, 7, 19, 30, 40, 107, 200
Syferfontein, 153-156, 160-161, 164, 200, 202-203
Tweebosch, 174-178, 187
Vallentin, 99-100, 133-135, 141
Van den Heever, 19, 100-101, 201
van Emmenes, 98, 100-103
Van Stadensrus, 114
Victoria Cross, 18-19, 21, 78, 83, 116, 152, 154-155, 158, 200, 202-203, 205
Victoria, 30, 32, 67, 69-70, 76-77, 79, 81, 83, 85, 123, 135
Viljoen, 8, 35, 49, 66-69, 71-72, 74-75, 78-80, 82, 91-93, 122, 124, 153-155, 192-193, 197, 202-203
Vlakfontein, 21, 82, 92, 115, 133, 143, 145-146, 153-156, 202-203, 205
Von Donop, 173, 175
Vryheid, 11-12, 14-15, 105, 125, 134-135, 165, 173
Wessels, 51, 109, 114-117, 120, 142, 190
White, 114, 116, 118, 135
Wilmansrust, 77, 79-80, 82-84, 92, 202
Wysfontein, 29-30